The New York Times

IN THE HEADLINES

Voter Suppression

BLOCKING THE BALLOT BOX

THE NEW YORK TIMES EDITORIAL STAFF

Published in 2021 by New York Times Educational Publishing
in association with The Rosen Publishing Group, Inc.
29 East 21st Street, New York, NY 10010

First Edition

The New York Times
Caroline Que: Editorial Director, Book Development
Cecilia Bohan: Photo Rights/Permissions Editor
Heidi Giovine: Administrative Manager

Rosen Publishing
Megan Kellerman: Managing Editor
Meredith Day: Editor
Brian Garvey: Art Director

Cataloging-in-Publication Data
Names: New York Times Company.
Title: Voter suppression: blocking the ballot box / edited by the
New York Times editorial staff.
Description: New York : New York Times Educational Publishing,
2021. | Series: In the headlines | Includes glossary and index.
Identifiers: ISBN 9781642824247 (library bound) | ISBN
9781642824230 (pbk.) | ISBN 9781642824254 (ebook)
Subjects: LCSH: Voting—United States—Juvenile literature. | Voter
registration—Corrupt practices—United States—Juvenile literature.
| Elections—Corrupt practices—United States—Juvenile literature.
| Election law—United States—Juvenile literature. | Suffrage—
United States—Juvenile literature. | Race discrimination—Political
aspects—United States—Juvenile literature. |
Minorities—Suffrage—United States—Juvenile literature.
Classification: LCC JK1846.V684 2021 | DDC 324.60973—dc23

Manufactured in the United States of America

On the cover: A sign directing voters to have a photo ID in
Arlington, Va., Nov. 4, 2014; Doug Mills/The New York Times.

Contents

CHAPTER 2

The Impact of Voter Fraud and ID Laws

CHAPTER 3

Other Voter Suppression Tactics

CHAPTER 4

The 2018 Georgia Governor's Race

CHAPTER 5

The Future of Voting

Introduction

THE RIGHT TO VOTE is a hallmark of democracy — it gives ordinary citizens the opportunity to choose who they want to represent their voice in government at all levels, from city council to president of the United States. But the reality of voting in the United States is much more complicated. Many surprising factors can affect who is able to cast a ballot on Election Day, long after some of the largest barriers to voting have been eliminated via federal law or amendment to the U.S. Constitution. Nationally, voters cannot be discriminated against for their sex or race; it is also illegal to require voters to pay a fee, or poll tax, in order to vote. But more subtle policies, many of which vary widely by state, can still make it difficult or impossible for someone to vote — and often, the voters who are most affected continue to be poor or members of minority communities, just as they were in the past.

States may have different rules about how to register to vote, including how far in advance of the election people must register. A major source of contention is the identification that voters need to present at the polls: States with stricter regulations are placing a greater burden on people who are less likely to have a driver's license or other state ID, such as students and elderly people. Getting the ID could itself be an arduous process if a person can't get time off work to stand in line, can't afford to pay a registration fee or doesn't have the proper documentation to prove who they are. On Election Day, unless they are eligible for an absentee ballot or have vote-by-mail in their state, voters need to get to the appropriate polling place, which may not be nearby or open during convenient hours for their work schedule. People who have moved or haven't voted in many years may find that local election officials have removed their name from the voting rolls. All of

Poll workers at a training session in Albany, N.Y., learn about the new voting technology that became a part of the state's early voting process in October 2019.

these barriers to voting can be discouraging and lead to lower voter turnout.

On the other hand, it's important to make sure that only eligible voters are participating. Like voter suppression, voter fraud has a long history. The most legendary example is in Chicago, where a 1983 Chicago Tribune investigation of one million votes found that 10 percent of them were fraudulent. The Democratic party machine in the city coordinated to cast ballots for thousands of dead people who were still on active lists of registered voters. But studies have consistently shown that in-person voter fraud is extremely rare: There is little risk of the same person voting multiple times or impersonating another voter at the polls.

In recent years, the debate about voter suppression versus voter fraud has been highly polarized. Democrats argue that voter-suppression tactics unfairly target disadvantaged groups: African-

Americans, Hispanics, impoverished neighborhoods, disabled people, elderly people and so on. Because of this, Democrats advocate for making voting easier and more available to all who are eligible through early voting periods, automatic voter registration and more flexible ID requirements. Meanwhile, Republicans maintain that strict regulations on voting, such as voter ID laws, are necessary to combat voter fraud and do not constitute an undue burden on voters. As both parties compete for votes and try to turn out people on their side, they may see an advantage in discouraging people who disagree with them from participating.

In the 2016 presidential race, Donald J. Trump forcefully argued that voter fraud was a serious and rampant problem, a charge he continued to make during his presidency despite a lack of evidence for it. Voters also began to fear that their votes would not be fairly counted after evidence emerged that Russia had conducted a targeted campaign to interfere in the 2016 presidential election — a troubling threat that remained throughout the 2018 midterm elections and in the lead-up to the 2020 race. The articles compiled here describe the various forms that voter suppression takes, as well as the efforts to combat it and ensure every eligible voter can exercise their rights.

CHAPTER 1

Groups Targeted by Voter Suppression

Historically, voter suppression tactics have focused on African-Americans. The Voting Rights Act of 1965 outlawed many of these tactics, but black, Hispanic, Native American and other minority voters are still often targeted. Other groups face obstacles as well, such as disabled voters who can't get to the polls. Also, college students often struggle to vote if their student IDs aren't considered an acceptable form of voter identification. Another question is when — or whether — to allow convicted felons to vote after they have completed their sentence.

16 Years After Bush v. Gore, Still Wrestling With Ballot-Box Rules

RETRO REPORT | **BY CLYDE HABERMAN** | **FEB. 21, 2016**

Retro Report re-examines the leading stories of decades past through essays and video documentaries.

REFLECTING ON BASEBALL ATTENDANCE, the philosopher Yogi Berra observed that "if people don't want to come to the ballpark, how are you going to stop them?" He could have said much the same thing about the American electorate. If voters don't want to go to the polls, what is going to stop them, too? Often enough, nothing has.

Across the decades, Americans have chosen not to exercise the franchise aerobically. The turnout rate in national elections, typically below 60 percent, ranks near the bottom among the world's developed democracies. The share of Americans who even bother registering to vote — 64.6 percent, according to the most recent figures from the United States Census Bureau — does not come close to rates exceeding 90 percent in Western Europe and Canada. Even in a supposedly banner year like 2008, when Barack Obama's candidacy generated plenty of excitement, the turnout was not quite 62 percent, a pace that countries like Belgium, Denmark and Sweden would regard as dismal.

Against that backdrop, decisions about who is eligible to vote and who is not can inflame political passions. It has been thus since the earliest days of the republic, but for the last decade or more the fires have burned fiercely. The spark? Bush v. Gore, the politically supercharged case that in 2000 produced one of the United States Supreme Court's most famous — some would say infamous — rulings. With the 2016 presidential race well underway, the consequences of Bush v. Gore are now examined by Retro Report, a series of video documentaries exploring major news stories of the past and their lasting impact.

A short version of this complex case is that the court rejected calls for a recount of extremely close Florida results in the 2000 presidential election. The justices' 5-to-4 vote broke along the ideological lines that are now receiving renewed scrutiny with the death of Justice Antonin Scalia.

The decision delivered Florida's 25 electoral votes to the Republican nominee, George W. Bush, handing him the narrowest of victories over his Democratic rival, Al Gore. By then, Florida's voting process had been exposed as a mess. Not that it was alone in this regard. Whatever their political loyalties, Americans had to face a raw reality: Their electoral system, the crown jewel of their democracy, was severely blemished and needed resetting.

The ostensible repair came in the form of the Help America Vote Act, passed overwhelmingly by both houses of Congress in 2002 and signed into law by President Bush. HAVA, as it was known, required states and municipalities to bring their election procedures into the

21st century, with electronic voting machines, improved methods of voter registration and better training of poll workers. But instead of an electoral nirvana, the new law ushered in an era of deep political contention, one that Retro Report succinctly describes as "voting wars."

HAVA left it to each state to work out the details of its new rules, and that allowed for some elastic definitions of fair play. Some states rewrote their laws in ways that made it tougher for many people to cast ballots. Others eased access to the polls. California and Oregon, for instance, have shifted the burden of voter registration from the citizen to the state. Their residents are now automatically registered whenever they get new drivers' licenses or have other routine dealings with government agencies.

While any generalization has its exceptions, it is reasonable to say that states imposing new restrictions are commonly those where Republicans dominate. States choosing to enhance ballot access — such as by increasing the number of days for early voting — are typically in the hands of Democrats.

Republicans say their lone goal is to protect the integrity of elections by eliminating voter fraud, which they describe as widespread and, ahem, conspicuous in Democratic-controlled cities and states. Their solutions include shrinking opportunities for early voting, eliminating Election Day registration, forbidding former prison inmates to vote and, most important, limiting the kinds of identification that voters must use to prove who they are.

The impact of these measures falls notably on the poor, the young, African-Americans, Latinos and other minorities — groups that usually vote for Democrats. Civil rights groups say blacks and Hispanics are blatantly made targets, given that they are less likely than others to have certain approved types of ID, like drivers' licenses or passports.

As for the allegation of systematic voter fraud, skeptics ask a simple question: Where is it? News organizations and others exploring this issue have found no evidence to support charges that the political process is commonly corrupted by unscrupulous people voting twice or passing themselves off as someone else.

Indeed, evidence is also scant that voter suppression has widely turned election results upside down.

Republican officials reject any suggestion that voter suppression is their true agenda. In what way, they ask, is a routine identity check unfair?

"I think voter identification is just a responsible act," Dennis K. Baxley, a Republican member of Florida's House of Representatives, told Retro Report. "If I go to a bank, I expect them to verify and protect my money and make sure I'm the one getting it."

The voter-war fires got a fresh infusion of oxygen in 2013 when the Supreme Court knocked out a core feature of the 1965 Voting Rights Act. This was a provision requiring nine states, most of them in the South, to get advance federal approval for any changes in their election laws. Those states, along with many counties and municipalities in other states, had histories of discrimination against minority voters. That "preclearance" requirement was deemed out of date and unjustified by the court (in yet another 5-to-4 vote that tracked the justices' ideological leanings).

In short order, some states passed more restrictive balloting laws. One of them was North Carolina, which, with its 15 electoral votes, looms ever larger these days as a battleground in presidential elections. In particular, national attention has focused on a North Carolina requirement that voters produce one of six accepted forms of identification, or else submit a provisional ballot. The state chapter of the N.A.A.C.P. has challenged the law in federal court, charging that this mandate is a barely disguised effort to disenfranchise many African-Americans and Latinos. Testimony ended this month. The outcome of the case may become a test of the juridical viability of other voting laws passed in recent years.

Still, legal arguments aside, the fact remains that one need not work terribly hard to suppress the vote in this country. It is virtually self-suppressing. In the 2014 midterm elections, the turnout among eligible voters was the lowest for any election cycle since World War II: a paltry 36.7 percent, according to the United States Elections Project.

One reason may involve tactics like gerrymandering, a refined art in the computer age that enables incumbents to render themselves and their political parties almost invincible. Analyzing this year's elections for the House of Representatives, The Cook Political Report has concluded that only 16 of the 435 seats qualify as true tossups.

"The framers of the Constitution would no doubt be shocked that so few members of the 'People's House' are actually held at risk in general elections," a bipartisan group called YouDrawTheLines2021 says on its website.

Or as Yogi might have put it, when people see no earthly reason to come out to vote, nothing can stop them.

The Supreme Court Ruled That Voting Restrictions Were a Bygone Problem. Early Voting Results Suggest Otherwise.

COLUMN | BY EMILY BAZELON | NOV. 7, 2016

TOMORROW, AND THE early voting leading up to it, mark the first presidential election since the Supreme Court clipped the protective wings of the Voting Rights Act. In 2013, speaking for a conservative majority of five, Chief Justice John Roberts effectively eliminated the safeguards created by a provision of the law called Section 5, saying that Congress could no longer require states and counties with a history of racial discrimination to get the approval of the Department of Justice before changing local voting rules and practices. Roberts said things had "changed dramatically" since the 1960s, and these jurisdictions, which are mostly in the South, didn't need oversight from the D.O.J. anymore. They could be trusted to treat minority voters fairly on their own.

As evidence of change, Roberts pointed to the end of the literacy test and other methods of barring voter registration, which included the poll tax. But his conservative majority didn't account for the hassle tax — the new price that minority voters disproportionately pay. In North Carolina over the weekend, people stood in line for hours in counties with large black and student populations. In a study of 381 counties covered by Section 5, about half the total number, the Leadership Conference Education Fund found 868 fewer places to vote than existed in 2012.

There are legitimate reasons to close a polling place, like saving money, while increasing access to voting by mail and early voting. But before the Supreme Court's 2013 ruling, the D.O.J. had the power to ensure that state and local voting boards did not use "budget cuts or voter modernization as cover to disenfranchise people of color," the L.C.E.F. study points out. "In a world without Section 5, that process — that protection for minority voters — has ceased."

And so voters of color are once again fighting for access to the most basic right of citizenship. When the Supreme Court heard arguments in the 2013 case, Shelby County v. Holder, experts predicted that the biggest impact of striking down Section 5 would be the cumulative effect of all the small stuff — "under the radar" local tinkering to district lines and polling locations and hours, as Heather Gerken, a Yale Law School professor, put it. When Section 5 was enforced, state and county officials chafed at submitting every alteration for federal approval. But the alternative is to resort to after-the-fact remedies. People are turned away from the polls, or purged from the rolls, or refused ID, and *then* these violations of their rights can be challenged.

Left to their own devices by the Supreme Court, some states and counties appear to be testing how far they can go with voter suppression. North Carolina is a case in point. Following the court's decision in Shelby County, the Republican-led Legislature passed a law stuffed with voting restrictions, including voter ID requirements and reductions in early voting. Last summer, the United States Court of Appeals for the Fourth Circuit struck down most of the law, finding that it targeted Democratic African-American voters "with almost surgical precision." Justifying a plan to end Sunday voting, the state said that counties allowing it in 2014 were "disproportionately black" and "disproportionately Democratic." The appeals court judges correctly called this "as close to a smoking gun as we are likely to see in modern times." The Republicans running the state wanted to change a voting practice out of concern that "African-Americans, who had overwhelmingly voted for Democrats, had too much access to the franchise."

The ruling, which restored a week of early voting, should have turned Republican lawmakers around. Instead, they started "pulling out all the stops to suppress the state's reliably Democratic black vote," wrote Ari Berman, author of the recent book "Give Us the

Ballot." County elections boards, which Republicans control, voted to cut the hours of early voting in Charlotte's Mecklenburg County, which Barack Obama won overwhelmingly in 2012, and where 70 percent of African-American voters voted early. Republicans denied the voter-suppression charges, saying they were simply trying, for partisan reasons not tied to race, to "rebalance the scales." Yet in a Monday news release, the state Republican Party highlighted the decrease in African-American early voting and the rise in the share of "Caucasian voters."

Before the Supreme Court's ruling in Shelby County, the elections boards would have had to make the neutral case for their preferred changes to the D.O.J. beforehand — and before expensive litigation. The same is true of a move by the secretary of state in Georgia to clean up the voter rolls. In 2014, the state criminally investigated voter-registration drives by Asian-American and African-American groups that registered 85,000 new voters and found problems with only 25 of the new registrants; no charges were filed. Over the next two years, Georgia canceled the registration of between 30,000 and 50,000 people for what turned out to be typographical and clerical errors.

Advocacy groups sued and won: 34,000 people are being restored to the rolls. But beginning in 2012, Georgia also changed the status of 372,000 more to inactive, which means that while they can vote, they don't receive mailings about how to vote from the state and they don't show up on the public lists used for get-out-the-vote efforts. Organizers aligned with communities of color, like the New Georgia Project, have tried to reach them; they won't know how successful they've been until the returns are in.

To Stacey Abrams, the house minority leader for the Georgia Assembly, it's clear that what's at stake is the balance of power. Georgia is 54 percent white, and the population of people of color is growing. "The challenged party, the Republicans, are trying to find a way to maintain a majority," she said. "Voter suppression has become incredibly inventive."

Abrams thinks the solution is to bring back the oversight role the D.O.J. used to play. "The only impediment to this type of behavior is to have a team from outside that understands the impact and sees the patterns," she said. The Supreme Court has the authority to resurrect protections like those in Section 5, perhaps for a new set of jurisdictions. In the last couple of election cycles, states like Ohio and Wisconsin, as well as Texas and Arizona, have stood out for their strict voter ID laws, or efforts to cut back on early voting, or other moves that tend to lower the minority vote. "I agree that the demography of America is very different than it was in the 1960s," Abrams said. "While the Voting Rights Act was passed in reaction to Jim Crow, the growing populations of people of color in this country live in different places than they did even a decade and a half ago." Protecting their rights requires a "more expansive reach." That kind of shift could come from a new Supreme Court. Or it could come from Congress in the form of a new Voting Rights Act. The likelihood of either is in the hands of the voters — the ones who can cast their ballots.

EMILY BAZELON is a staff writer for the magazine and the Truman Capote fellow at Yale Law School.

Black Turnout in Alabama Complicates Debate on Voting Laws

BY ALAN BLINDER AND MICHAEL WINES | DEC. 24, 2017

MONTGOMERY, ALA. — Even before a defiant Roy S. Moore stood at a lectern this month and refused to concede the Alabama Senate race, one political reality was clear: An extraordinary turnout among black voters had helped push Doug Jones to a rare Democratic victory in this state.

That turnout, in which registered black voters appeared to cast ballots at a higher rate than white ones, has become the most recent reference point in the complicated picture about race and elections laws.

At issue, at a time when minorities are becoming an increasingly powerful slice of the electorate, is how much rules like Alabama's voter ID law serve as a brake on that happening. The turnout by black voters in Alabama raises a question: Did it come about because voting restrictions were not as powerful as critics claim or because voters showed up in spite of them?

Whether blacks and other minorities vote has become an evermore crucial element in the national political calculus. Minority voters, who lean overwhelmingly Democratic, were 29 percent of eligible voters in 2012 and 31 percent in 2016; by 2020, the figure is expected to rise to nearly 34 percent.

LaTosha Brown, an Alabama native and a founder of the Black Voters Matter Fund, which backed voter-mobilization efforts in the Senate contest, said the impact of voter suppression in Alabama was real, but that the policies were sometimes a motivating factor.

"Historically and traditionally, there has been a strong voice of resistance to those that are undemocratic," she said. "I don't think that this is new; I think that has always been the role that black voters, particularly in the Deep South, have played."

A polling station in Brundidge, Ala. Research, particularly of voter ID laws in Texas, Wisconsin and other states, offers an imprecise picture of how much ID laws have suppressed turnout.

But research, particularly of voter ID laws in Texas, Wisconsin and other states, provides an imprecise picture of how much similar laws suppress turnout. And Eitan Hersh, a Tufts University political scientist who contributed to the analysis of Texas' strict voter ID law, said research indicated that voter ID laws could alter very close elections but might not be as influential as some critics claim.

"These laws are complicated to assess," Mr. Hersh said. "Alabama was a place where there was a lot of campaigning, and when campaigns liven up, you have a lot of mobilization efforts" that could offset the effect of an ID law on turnout.

Alabama, where a bloody history of battling for the right to vote gave birth to the Voting Rights Act of 1965, and a lawsuit led to the 2013 Supreme Court case that dramatically weakened the law, is seldom described as a model for voting rules.

Like only 12 other states, Alabama does not permit early voting, which is disproportionately used by minorities and the poor. Its restrictions on voting by people with felony records were recently relaxed, but remain among the nation's toughest and likely curb black turnout. The state's voter ID law, which was challenged in federal court, threatened to disenfranchise at least 100,000 registered voters, many of them black or Hispanic, according to the N.A.A.C.P. Legal Defense Fund. And a panel of federal judges ruled this year that 12 state legislative districts had been gerrymandered to dilute African-American voting power. The congressional map is also gerrymandered.

Since 2010, 23 states, mostly under Republican control, have enacted laws requiring voters to show identification before casting ballots, all in the name of curbing a voter-fraud threat that almost all experts and election officials say is largely mythical. Six states have reduced early voting days or hours, seven have stiffened requirements to register and three states have made it harder for people with felony convictions to regain the right to vote.

A lawsuit challenging aggressive purging of voter rolls in Ohio, where thousands of legitimate voters have been removed from the rolls, will next month go before the United States Supreme Court; the case could give similar plans a red or green light. The court is also considering arguments over the constitutionality of partisan gerrymandering, which computer technology has turned into an evermore powerful tool.

On the other hand, in many states, most of them divided or Democratic leaning, access to the franchise continues to expand: Since 2015, nine states have passed laws to automatically register new voters when they interact with government agencies. Colorado, Oregon and Washington have moved almost entirely to mail-in ballots and turnout has bumped upward as a result. Nearly three-quarters of states allow early voting, no-excuse absentee voting, or both.

In the Alabama vote, there were reports of scattered troubles, including technology problems, voter ID disputes, issues with voters improperly classified as inactive and long lines at many polling places.

A billboard near Midland City, Ala. The state has a history of voter suppression, but African-American residents made the difference in the recent Senate election.

But the gravest fears of Alabama's critics were not realized. Some of that reflected years of advocacy by voting rights groups, including the concerted pushback that led the state, in 2015, to back away from a plan to close 31 driver's license offices in rural areas, many of them predominantly black.

Alabama's secretary of state, John H. Merrill, said allegations of irregularities, from the left and right, in the Dec. 12 election were not borne out. "It's just people making things up, and they think they can because of what they've observed that happened before or what our history has been," said Mr. Merrill, a Republican.

Still unclear is what role voting restrictions, including voter ID, are playing on turnout here and elsewhere. Exit polls are preliminary, but the ones available in Alabama suggest the share of blacks who cast ballots — roughly 41 percent of the African-Americans voters — exceeding the 35 or so percent of whites who turned out. The divide likely reflects a robust black turnout and modest participation from whites who were unenthusiastic about Mr. Moore, whose already-controversial candidacy was dogged by accusations of sexual misconduct.

One recent academic study concluded that the historic turnout gap between white and minority voters increased sharply — as much as fivefold — in states with the strictest voter ID laws, producing a "clear partisan distortion" favoring Republicans.

In Texas, where federal courts have invalidated parts of one of the nation's toughest ID laws, a detailed analysis concluded that 3.6 percent of white registered voters in Texas lacked any legally acceptable ID — and 5.7 percent of Hispanic voters, and 7.5 percent of African-Americans. But among more likely voters who cast ballots in the 2010 and 2012 elections, only 1.4 percent lacked a valid ID. An estimated 600,000 registered voters lacked a photo ID that qualified them to vote under the law.

Still other studies in Texas and Wisconsin concluded that confusion over voter ID laws meant that more people who actually had valid IDs but believed they did not stayed home on Election Day than did voters who actually lacked identification.

The Wisconsin study suggested it was mathematically possible — though far from certain — that the number of voters who stayed home in the 2016 general election exceeded Donald J. Trump's 22,748-vote margin of victory there. Some critics of voter restrictions took that as proof of the impact of such laws, but among scholars, caution is more the rule.

"It depends on where, and it depends on who," said Justin Levitt, a professor at Loyola Law School in Los Angeles who also oversaw voting-rights issues in the Obama administration Justice Department. "There are real, live instances where positions are taken to keep eligible people from showing up at the polls or to make it needlessly harder to vote. But it's not nationwide, and it's not all the time."

Benard Simelton, the president of the Alabama branch of the N.A.A.C.P., said he believed that the voter ID law had led some people, many of them poor, to stop trying to participate in elections at all.

"As long as that's a requirement, what are people to do if they haven't been able to obtain the required voter ID?" Mr. Simelton said. "My gut tells me that people who don't have it have given up."

Some voting rights advocates stress that the relevant measure should be whether people were unable to vote, not whether particular policies determined the outcome of the election.

"Voter suppression might not be attributable in every instance to changing an election outcome, but it's significant to people who have barriers in front of them at the ballot box," said Myrna Pérez, the deputy director of the democracy program at the Brennan Center for Justice at the New York University School of Law. She added: "The country is going to be poorer if we only care about voter suppression when it affects the outcome."

The outcome, however, is increasingly the standard by which voting-rights cases are decided. The Supreme Court's Shelby County v. Holder decision, which dramatically scaled back the Voting Rights Act, relieved scores of states and local governments with a history of bias from the need to prove that new election rules did not discriminate. Since 2013, the burden of proving discrimination — and the cost of detecting and litigating it — has been shifted to minority voters and the groups that represent them.

To many, that's a standard that rankles.

"I do think that very committed, focused people will find a way" to cast ballots, said Ms. Brown, the co-founder of the Black Voters Matter Fund. "But is that fair? If you put a rock on my foot and I beat you in the race, that still doesn't make it O.K. that you put a rock on my foot."

ALAN BLINDER reported from Montgomery, and MICHAEL WINES from Washington. JESS BIDGOOD contributed reporting from Dothan, Ala.

What the Supreme Court Doesn't Get About Racism

EDITORIAL | BY THE NEW YORK TIMES | APRIL 2, 2018

The editorial board represents the opinions of the board, its editor and the publisher. It is separate from the newsroom and the Op-Ed section.

IN THE LAST SPEECH of his life, on April 3, 1968, in Memphis, the Rev. Dr. Martin Luther King Jr. laid out the case for the dignity and equality of African-Americans as simply as he could. "We aren't engaged in any negative protest and in any negative arguments with anybody. We are saying that we are determined to be men. We are determined to be people," he said. "All we say to America is, 'Be true to what you said on paper.' "

The moral clarity of that appeal is bracing, and so is the difficulty of achieving it — a fact that is evident nowhere as much as in the fight for voting rights. As Dr. King knew well, the history of voting in the United States was, and is, in large part the history of white people in power devising endless ways to keep black people from casting a ballot.

It's been true all along, from the complete disenfranchisement of slavery to the effective silencing of the Jim Crow era up to now, when a welter of clever and at times subtle laws operates to make it harder for minorities to get to the polls, and to have an equal voice — or any voice at all — in the choice of our representatives and policies.

This is always a serious matter, but especially now, as the midterm elections approach with control of Congress at stake. As recent elections in Virginia and Alabama have shown, minority voters can make all the difference.

Dr. King understood this half a century ago, which is why he considered the right to vote the centerpiece of the civil rights movement. "Voting is the foundation stone for political action," he wrote in an essay titled "Civil Right No. 1," which ran in The New York Times

Magazine in March 1965, days after the march and bloodshed in Selma and months before the Voting Rights Act would become law.

The right to vote wasn't just "the most fundamental of all privileges of democracy," Dr. King wrote; it would, if truly enjoyed by black Americans, transform the entire country. "Our vote would place in Congress true representatives of the people who would legislate for the Medicare, housing, schools and jobs required by all men of any color."

The Voting Rights Act of 1965 is arguably the most popular and effective civil rights law in the nation's history. Soon after it passed, black registration and turnout skyrocketed. In Mississippi, 7 percent of eligible black voters were registered in 1965; two years later, 60 percent were. Still, the law shouldn't have been necessary. The constitutional amendments it codified had been passed about a century earlier but then were systematically undermined by a racist regime determined to protect white power. And even though Congress has reauthorized the law four times — the last time, in 2006, the Senate approved it 98 to 0 — it still requires frequent care and tending by the federal courts, especially the Supreme Court.

Unfortunately, the court's conservative majority has severely weakened the protections the law was intended to provide. The biggest blow came in a 2013 decision, Shelby County v. Holder. In that case, the five conservative justices, led by Chief Justice John Roberts Jr., gutted the heart of the act, which identified several states with long histories of voting discrimination, most in the South, and required them to get federal permission before changing their voting laws. While that remedy may have been a necessary response to 1960s-era racism, the chief justice wrote, "things have changed dramatically."

In one sense, he was right: Racial discrimination in voting is no longer as blatant or systemic as it was in 1965. But the idea that the American fixation on race and power had magically evaporated in just a few decades was, at best, strikingly naïve. It was also disproved within hours of the court's ruling, when Republican lawmakers in

Texas and North Carolina, both states that had been covered by the Voting Rights Act, rammed through discriminatory new voting laws that they had been gunning to pass for years, including some that had been blocked under the act.

If this wasn't enough evidence that things have not, in fact, changed dramatically, the point was driven home by the election of Donald Trump in 2016, and the resurgence of overt racism and white nationalism that has followed, with no meaningful pushback from the president.

In the years before Mr. Trump's election and in the time since, Republican lawmakers around the country aggressively pushed through laws to make voting harder for certain groups, particularly minorities. Poll taxes and literacy tests have given way to voter-ID laws, cutbacks to early voting and same-day registration, polling place closings, voter-roll purges, racially discriminatory redistricting and felon disenfranchisement laws — most of which, though justified on race-neutral grounds, harm minority voters more.

They can also depress turnout, when voters who are not in fact blocked from voting become discouraged by a state apparatus that exudes hostility toward their attempts to exercise their fundamental right.

Are these laws, passed almost invariably by Republican lawmakers, intentionally racist? Or are they merely taking partisan advantage of the fact that black people today vote overwhelmingly for Democrats? It shouldn't matter. Either way, black voters are targeted, their right to vote hampered.

In the past couple of years, lower federal courts — notably in Texas, Wisconsin and North Carolina, home to some of the worst voting laws in the country — have begun to recognize this. They have become more skeptical of lawmakers' rationales for passing voting restrictions and have zeroed in on the real impact of such laws on minorities and other vulnerable groups. In striking down a remarkably harsh North Carolina law in 2016, the United States Court of Appeals for the Fourth

Circuit found that lawmakers had targeted black voters "with almost surgical precision."

This is an important step toward a robust judicial defense of voting rights. Now Congress must repair the damage the Supreme Court inflicted on the Voting Rights Act. The most important fix is to restore and strengthen the federal government's oversight of states and localities that continue to discriminate in voting. This would stop bad laws before they could take effect. It would also eliminate the years of delays that are part of most election-related litigation.

Fifty years after his death, Dr. King's message is as urgent as it ever was: Justice delayed is justice denied. That may be the most insidious legacy of the court's Shelby County decision. Lawmakers get free rein to discriminate, while citizens must file private lawsuits and then wait, often years, while elections keep being held, representatives keep getting elected and policies keep getting made.

The Supreme Court has two options. It can follow the lead of the lower federal courts and be more honest about discriminatory voting laws, or it can stick with the willful blindness of its 2013 ruling and let discrimination flourish.

To make the right choice, the justices need only look to someone like Representative John Lewis, the 16-term Georgia congressman who was nearly beaten to death while marching in Selma. Or they can look to Dr. King himself, who would have turned 89 in January. America was legally an apartheid state in living memory. That fact should serve as a corrective to the dangerous notion that "things have changed" enough in the short time since to let our guard down.

Whose Votes Really Count?

REVIEW | BY JENNIFER SZALAI | SEPT. 12, 2018

One Person, No Vote:
How Voter Suppression Is Destroying Our Democracy
By Carol Anderson
271 pages. Bloomsbury. $27.

AS THE ELABORATE POST-MORTEM of the presidential election drags on — amid all the diagnoses of Russian interference, Clintonian blunders and white-working-class resentment — Carol Anderson wants to direct your attention to one simple fact: In November 2016, black voter turnout fell by 7 percent.

Anderson rebukes anyone who takes this as a facile statement of how black voters felt about Hillary Clinton. "Minority voters did not just refuse to show up," she writes in "One Person, No Vote: How Voter Suppression Is Destroying Our Democracy." "Republican legislatures and governors systematically blocked African-Americans, Hispanics and Asian-Americans from the polls."

The 2016 presidential election was the first in 50 years to be held without the full protections of the Voting Rights Act. Three years before, in 2013, the Supreme Court had revoked the part of the law that required states with a history of voting discrimination to get federal approval in order to change their voting statutes. The ruling effectively left voters at the mercy of state legislators. Some of these law makers, like the Republican Party itself, didn't draw significant support from minority communities. So in the interests of self-preservation, Anderson says, they changed the laws in ways that made it harder for minorities to vote. President Donald J. Trump is just one result; a profound and polarizing distortion of American democracy is another.

Anderson's argument isn't new. Ari Berman, the author of the excellent "Give Us the Ballot" (2015), has been making a similar case to anyone who will listen. His book also included original reporting, and interviews with lawyers, activists and government officials who experienced the implementation of the 1965 Voting Rights Act firsthand.

Anderson, a professor of African-American studies at Emory University, has written a slender volume that is one part historical primer and one part spirited manifesto, and is clearly timed for the midterms. (Don't let the number of pages fool you; more than 100 of them are for endnotes. Anderson has a distracting tendency to quote even basic factual phrases — like "the State's federal public housing residents" — instead of simply stating or rewording them.)

"One Person, No Vote" reads like a speedy sequel of sorts to her previous book, the elegant and illuminating best-seller "White Rage" (2016), which traced how periods of black progress have so often triggered a backlash that "wreaks havoc subtly, almost imperceptibly" through the legislatures and courts. "White rage doesn't have to wear sheets, burn crosses or take to the streets," she wrote. "Working the halls of power, it can achieve its ends far more effectively, far more destructively."

Her new book seems to have been written from a state of emergency, in an adrenaline-fueled sprint. Anderson is a stinging polemicist; her book rolls through a condensed history of voting rights and disenfranchisement, without getting bogged down in legislative minutiae. This is harder than it looks; as Anderson explains, it's often through legislative minutiae that voting rights are curtailed.

The lurid violence of voter suppression looms large in the public imagination, but ever since black men were granted the franchise in the wake of the Civil War, politicians have also devised discriminatory rules "dressed up in the genteel garb of bringing 'integrity' to the voting booth." Before the Voting Rights Act took effect, poll taxes and literacy tests were the favored methods of voter suppression; they have since been replaced by gerrymandering and extreme measures to combat the phantom menace of voter fraud.

The trick is to keep everything constitutional, Anderson says, staying within the boundaries of the 14th and 15th Amendments, which promised "equal protection" and barred discrimination "on account of race." As the Virginia politician Carter Glass put it candidly in 1902, "Discrimination! Why, that is precisely what we propose." It was, he said, an elected official's duty "to discriminate to the very extremity of permissible action under the limitations of the Federal Constitution, with a view to the elimination of every negro voter who can be gotten rid of, legally."

Contemporary rhetoric isn't so frank and incendiary. Anderson describes Georgia's Exact Match system and the Interstate Crosscheck as modern incarnations of old efforts to restrict the vote. Cloaked in anodyne phrases like "voter roll maintenance," those database-matching programs "gave the illusion of being clean, clinical, efficient and fair," Anderson writes, when in fact they had a "horrific effect on voter registration, especially for minorities." Tiny typographical errors triggered wrongful purges of eligible voters. According to one team of researchers, the Crosscheck program — which was vastly expanded by Kansas Secretary of State Kris Kobach, a staunch Trump ally currently running to be the state's governor — had an astonishing error rate of 99 percent.

From the perspective of federal enforcement, Anderson says, the situation for minority voters is looking even more perilous now than a couple of years ago. The Department of Justice under Attorney General Jeff Sessions — who as a United States attorney in Alabama tried (and failed) to obtain a conviction of three African-American activists for voter fraud and once called the Voting Rights Act "an intrusive piece of legislation" — has demanded that no fewer than 44 states detail their programs for, yes, voter roll maintenance. The Presidential Advisory Commission on Election Integrity (after reading this book, you won't be able look at the word "integrity" the same way again) is chaired by two figures who presided over aggressive anti-voter-fraud measures in their home states: Kobach and Vice President Mike Pence.

But at the grass-roots level, Anderson believes that things might be looking up. She offers a surprisingly riveting play-by-play of last year's special senate election in Alabama, in which Doug Jones, a Democrat, won a startling upset over the Republican Roy Moore. She concedes that Moore, buffeted by allegations of sexual assault, was an especially unappealing candidate, whatever one's politics. But she also shows how groups like the N.A.A.C.P. mobilized local efforts to help people register to vote and — in a state where poll closures made even getting to the voting booths an issue — to offer crucial transportation.

Behind the tactics deployed by both sides looms a larger question: What kind of future should this country pursue? Should it be a democracy that is, in Anderson's words, "vibrant, responsive and inclusive"? Or should it be a system that maximizes "the frustration of millions of citizens to minimize their participation in the electoral process"? To that end, this trenchant little book will push you to think not just about the vote count but about who counts, too.

The Student Vote Is Surging. So Are Efforts to Suppress It.

BY MICHAEL WINES | OCT. 24, 2019

The share of college students casting ballots doubled from 2014 to 2018, a potential boon to Democrats. But in Texas and elsewhere, Republicans are erecting roadblocks to the polls.

AUSTIN, TEXAS — At Austin Community College, civics is an unwritten part of the curriculum — so much so that for years the school has tapped its own funds to set up temporary early-voting sites on nine of its 11 campuses.

No more, however. This spring, the Texas Legislature outlawed polling places that did not stay open for the entire 12-day early-voting period. When the state's elections take place in three weeks, those nine sites — which logged many of the nearly 14,000 ballots that full-time students cast last year — will be shuttered. So will six campus polling places at colleges in Fort Worth, two in Brownsville, on the Mexico border, and other polling places at schools statewide.

"It was a beautiful thing, a lot of people out there in those long lines," said Grant Loveless, a 20-year-old majoring in psychology and political science who voted last November at a campus in central Austin. "It would hurt a lot of students if you take those polling places away."

The story at Austin Community College is but one example of a political drama playing out nationwide: After decades of treating elections as an afterthought, college students have begun voting in force.

Their turnout in the 2018 midterms — 40.3 percent of 10 million students tracked by Tufts University's Institute for Democracy & Higher Education — was more than double the rate in the 2014 midterms, easily exceeding an already robust increase in national turnout. Energized by issues like climate change and the Trump presidency, students have suddenly emerged as a potentially crucial voting bloc in the 2020 general election.

And almost as suddenly, Republican politicians around the country are throwing up roadblocks between students and voting booths.

Not coincidentally, the barriers are rising fastest in political battlegrounds and places like Texas where one-party control is eroding. Students lean strongly Democratic: In a March poll by the Institute of Politics at Harvard University's Kennedy School of Government, 45 percent of college students ages 18-24 identified as Democrats, compared to 29 percent who called themselves independents and 24 percent Republicans.

Some states have wrestled with voting eligibility for out-of-state students in the past. And the politicians enacting the roadblocks often say they are raising barriers to election fraud, not ballots. "The threat to election integrity in Texas is real, and the need to provide additional safeguards is increasing," the state's attorney general, Ken Paxton, said last year in announcing one of his office's periodic crackdowns on illegal voting. But evidence of widespread fraud is nonexistent, and the restrictions fit an increasingly unabashed pattern of Republican politicians' efforts to discourage voters likely to oppose them.

"Efforts to deprive any American of a convenient way to vote will have a chilling effect on voting," Nancy Thomas, the director of the Tufts institute, said. "And efforts to chill college students' voting are despicable — and very frustrating."

The headline example is in New Hampshire. There, a Republican-backed law took effect this fall requiring newly registered voters who drive to establish "domicile" in the state by securing New Hampshire driver's licenses and auto registrations, which can cost hundreds of dollars annually.

The dots are not hard to connect: According to the Tufts study, six in 10 New Hampshire college students come from outside the state, a rate among the nation's highest. As early as 2011, the state's Republican House speaker at the time, William O'Brien, promised to clamp down on unrestricted voting by students, calling them "kids voting liberal, voting their feelings, with no life experience."

Florida's Republican secretary of state outlawed early-voting sites at state universities in 2014, only to see 60,000 voters cast on-campus ballots in 2018 after a federal court overturned the ban. This year, the State Legislature effectively reinstated it, slipping a clause into a new elections law that requires all early-voting sites to offer "sufficient non-permitted parking" — an amenity in short supply on densely packed campuses.

North Carolina Republicans enacted a voter ID law last year that recognized student identification cards as valid — but its requirements proved so cumbersome that major state universities were unable to comply. A later revision relaxed the rules, but much confusion remains, and fewer than half the state's 180-plus accredited schools have sought to certify their IDs for voting.

Wisconsin Republicans also have imposed tough restrictions on using student IDs for voting purposes. The state requires poll workers to check signatures only on student IDs, although some schools issuing modern IDs that serve as debit cards and dorm room keys have removed signatures, which they consider a security risk.

The law also requires that IDs used for voting expire within two years, while most college ID cards have four-year expiration dates. And even students with acceptable IDs must show proof of enrollment before being allowed to vote.

"Universities have had to decide one by one whether they want to modify their IDs to make them acceptable, issue a second ID for voting purposes or do nothing," said Barry Burden, the director of the Elections Research Center at the University of Wisconsin-Madison. "And they've all gone in different directions."

While legislators call the rules anti-fraud measures, Wisconsin has not recorded a case of intentional student voter fraud in memory, Mr. Burden said. But a healthy turnout of legitimate student voters could easily tip the political balance in many closely divided states.

Senator Maggie Hassan of New Hampshire, a Democrat, won election in 2016 by 1,017 votes over her Republican rival, Kelly Ayotte. Gov.

Roy Cooper of North Carolina, a Democrat, won that year by about 10,000 votes in a state with nearly 500,000 undergraduates. And Donald J. Trump carried Wisconsin by fewer than 23,000 votes; the University of Wisconsin system alone enrolls more than 170,000 students.

Some critics suggest that opposition to campus-voting restrictions is overblown — that students can find other IDs to establish their identities, that campus polling sites are a luxury not afforded other voters.

But local election officials generally put polls where they are needed most, in packed places like universities and apartment complexes or locations like nursing homes where access is difficult.

Repeated studies have shown that making voting convenient improves turnout. And while it is difficult to say with certainty what causes turnout to decline, anecdotal evidence suggests that barriers to student voting have done just that. Nationwide, student turnout in the 2016 presidential election exceeded that of the 2012 presidential vote — but according to the Tufts institute, it fell sharply in Wisconsin, where the state's voter ID law first applied to students that year.

Hurdles to student voting are hardly limited to politically competitive states. Most notably, the voter ID law in deeply Republican Tennessee does not recognize student ID cards as valid for voting, and legislators have removed out-of-state driver's licenses from the list of valid identifications.

A Tennessee law requiring election officials to help register high school students is commonly skirted via a loophole, said Lisa Quigley, the top aide to Representative Jim Cooper, a Tennessee Democrat and voting rights advocate. And cities like Nashville and Knoxville, with large concentrations of college students, have no campus early voting polling places, she said.

Tennessee ranks 50th in voter turnout among the states and the District of Columbia. "We're terrible at voting," Ms. Quigley said. "And it's intentional."

Only Texas' turnout is worse. And as in Tennessee, voting is particularly difficult for the young.

Texas law requires educators to distribute voter registration forms to high school students, but the requirement appears to be ignored by most of the state's 3,700 secondary schools. And while many states allow students to preregister at 16 or 17, and even vote in primaries if they turn 18 by Election Day in November, Texas bars students from registering until two months before their 18th birthday, the nation's most restrictive rule.

The state's voter ID law — among the most onerous, though softened by court rulings — still excludes college and university ID cards and only allows the use of out-of-state driver's licenses that many students carry if voters sign a form swearing that they couldn't reasonably acquire an accepted ID and explaining why.

Some Texas schools have sought for years to lower those barriers. At the University of Texas at Austin, a group called TX Votes has greatly increased turnout by rallying students against voting restrictions and enlisting scores of campus groups in voting and registration campaigns.

Austin Community College, whose 39,000 full-time and 33,000 part-time students sprawl over campuses in four Texas counties, pursues a similar strategy. The system's student body is drawn largely from working-class and minority families.

In addition to sponsoring the campus voting, it gives its employees two hours off during every election to cast ballots.

It is not the only Texas college to set up campus voting. North of Austin, Southwestern University collected ballots from more than half of its 1,500 students last November in a one-day visit by a mobile polling place. Tarrant County, whose largest city is Fort Worth, racked up 11,000 votes at mobile campus sites; Cameron County, in southern Texas, opened three campus sites and reaped nearly 2,800 votes.

Dollar for dollar, mobile voting sites were "the most effective program we had," Dana DeBeauvoir, the Travis County clerk and chief elections official, said.

State legislators took a dimmer view. Last spring, State Representative Greg Bonnen, a Republican from suburban Houston, filed legislation to require that all polling places remain open during the whole early-voting period, eliminating pop-up polls. He argued that local politicians were using the sites to attract supportive voters for pet projects like school bond issues.

The Texas Association of Election Administrators opposed the change, and Democratic legislators proposed to exclude college campuses, nursing homes and other sites from the requirement. But Republicans rejected the changes and passed the bill on largely party-line votes.

There are efforts to push back at the restrictions on student voting. The elections administrator in Dallas County, Toni Pippins-Poole, decided after the Legislature outlawed temporary polls to spend the money needed to make pop-up voting sites on eight college campuses permanent.

In New Hampshire, the state chapter of the American Civil Liberties Union is suing to undo the State Legislature's domicile law. The League of Women Voters and the Andrew Goodman Foundation, a Mahwah, N.J., nonprofit group focused on protecting voting rights for young people, are contesting Florida's parking requirements for polls in federal court.

Purdue University said last month that it would temporarily not charge out-of-state students a fee for ID cards, which are valid for voting in Indiana. Mitchell E. Daniels Jr., Purdue's president and the state's Republican governor from 2005 to 2013, said he wanted to encourage civic literacy among students.

Advocates for student voters argue that those are the exceptions.

"Everyone 18 years and older has a right, if not a duty, to participate in our electoral system," said Maxim Thorne, the managing director of the Goodman Foundation. "We should be having conversations about how to make it easier, how to make it more welcoming, how to make it worthy of our time and effort. And what we're seeing is the reverse."

MICHAEL WINES writes about voting and other election-related issues. Since joining The Times in 1988, he has covered the Justice Department, the White House, Congress, Russia, southern Africa, China and various other topics.

For Native Americans, a 'Historic Moment' on the Path to Power at the Ballot Box

BY JULIE TURKEWITZ | JAN. 4, 2018

Court battles playing out over indigenous voting rights have the potential to tip tight races in states with large native populations and to influence matters of national importance.

SAN JUAN COUNTY, UTAH — In this county of desert and sagebrush, Wilfred Jones has spent a lifetime angered by what his people are missing. Running water, for one. Electricity, for another. But worst of all, in his view, is that the Navajo people here lack adequate political representation.

So Mr. Jones sued, and in late December, after a federal judge ruled that San Juan County's longtime practice of packing Navajo voters into one voting district violated the United States Constitution, the county was ordered to draw new district lines for local elections.

The move could allow Navajo people to win two of three county commission seats for the first time, overturning more than a century of political domination by white residents. And the shift here is part of an escalating battle over Native American enfranchisement, one that comes amid a larger wave of voting rights movements spreading across the country.

"It's a historic moment for us," said Mr. Jones, during a drive on the county's roller coaster dirt roads. "We look at what happened with the Deep South," he went on, "how they accomplished what they have. We can do the same thing."

The county is challenging the decision, arguing that the maps ordered by Judge Robert J. Shelby unconstitutionally consider race, and so discriminate against white voters.

"In one of the poorest counties in the nation, the last thing we need is to be constantly sued by these predatory attorneys," said Phil

Ms. Coggeshell's granddaughter, Kolela, catches the school bus in the southern part of Utah's San Juan County. The 10-mile trip takes over an hour, in part because of the poor road conditions.

Lyman, a county commissioner. "Outside people try to put this into a racial divide that simply doesn't exist in San Juan County."

Fights over indigenous voting rights are playing out in the West and the Midwest, a trend that has the potential to tip tight races in states with large native populations, like Alaska and Arizona, and to influence matters of national importance, like the future of Bears Ears National Monument, a conservation area in this county that is at the center of a fierce debate over public lands.

Today, Native Americans are suing over a new voter identification law in North Dakota, where lawyers say there is not a single driver's license site on a reservation in a state that requires identification to vote. The outcome of the lawsuit could influence this year's congressional election, helping to secure or flip the seat of Senator Heidi Heitkamp, a Democrat with wide Native American support.

In the battleground state of Nevada, the Pyramid Lake and Walker River Paiutes won a lawsuit in late 2016 that charged that tribal citizens had to travel as many as 100 miles to vote. The suit forced officials to open new polling stations in tribal areas and spurred nine other tribes to request their own election sites.

And in Alaska, where native people make up a fifth of the population, officials recently rolled out election materials in the Yup'ik, Inupiaq and Gwich'in languages, following federal rulings that found the state had failed to provide materials equivalent to those used by English speakers.

After those changes, turnout in villages rose by as much as 20 percent, increasing the political power of the state's native residents.

Other native voting cases are proceeding or have been recently settled in Arizona, Montana, South Dakota and Wyoming. And a second case is open in San Juan County, this one challenging the county's decision to move to an all-mail ballot. Plaintiffs contend this disenfranchises native people who live far from reliable mail service.

"It's part of a larger political trend of Native Americans organizing and protecting themselves," said Daniel McCool, a professor emeritus at the University of Utah and a voting rights expert who was hired by the plaintiffs in the Navajo redistricting case.

There are 6.6 million American Indians and Alaska Natives in the United States, representing about 2 percent of the population. But many live in America's most remote places — amid mountain passes or miles of near-empty plains — and the native path to the ballot box has often been less visible than that of other groups.

It was not until 1924 that Congress granted native people the right to vote, and for generations afterward, local and state governments have blocked them from doing so, often saying that Native Americans living on reservations were not state residents.

The Voting Rights Act of 1965 was a critical moment, prohibiting election practices that discriminate on the basis of race. But relatively few lawsuits were filed on behalf of native voters until the 1990s.

The pace of legal challenges has picked up recently, something observers attribute to a realization that American Indians can influence local and national policy. The fate of Bears Ears, a conservation area that originally occupied a quarter of this 8,000-square-mile county, is one such issue.

When President Trump slashed the size of the monument last month, one argument was that he was considering the desires of local officials. A Navajo-controlled commission, however, could oppose the decision, a move that could influence coming legal battles over the monument's fate.

San Juan County is a hardscrabble expanse in the state's southeast corner, and home to some 16,000 people. The county population is about half Native American and half white, and battles over resources have often fallen along racial lines.

The lower portion of the county overlaps the Navajo reservation, and native people bring millions of dollars to the county each year in the form of oil and gas revenue and other taxes. But those living on the reservation do not pay property taxes, frustrating many others who feel they pay more than their fair share.

In the south, where most native families live, the library is in the corner of a trailer, there is no hospital or bank, and residents have spent more than a generation suing the county for services.

Alicia Coggeshell, 52, lives in the south with two children and three grandchildren. She has no running water or internet service, and on a recent morning she traveled to the footbridge she uses to get to the market.

These days, it is so dilapidated that her neighbors sometimes fall into the icy water below, she said.

"We asked the county and the county says, It's not our responsibility. This is what we mean: forgotten," she said.

White families live mostly in the north, home to two expansive libraries, a community center on a golf course, a recreation center with a pool, and the seats of local power: the sheriff's office, the courthouse, the school administration building.

Tauna Larson, a retired educator who lives in the north, said she looked at the possibility of two Navajo commissioners with some trepidation. "I worry that they might tend to look out more for the reservation," she said. "The majority tends to take care of their own."

The county also has a contentious relationship with the federal government, which controls 60 percent of the land here and has battled with local leaders over a range of issues, including the protection of Native American artifacts and access to a beloved public canyon.

Commissioner Bruce Adams and Commissioner Lyman have been intensely critical of the federal government, and both said they believed the judge's decision was a punishment for their resistance.

"I think there is retribution," Mr. Adams said. "We're tired of being the scapegoat, saying we're doing everything wrong, when we try to abide by the law."

Judge Shelby declined to comment.

The old commission map made Native Americans about 30 percent of the population in two districts, and 93 percent in a third district. The new one makes them 66 percent in one district, 80 percent in another, and 11 percent in another.

It will be used in a 2018 local election.

Mr. Jones, the plaintiff in the case, is 62 and was born before most Native Americans could vote in the state.

On a recent evening he pulled on a black cowboy hat and walked into a tribal meeting to explain the results of the lawsuit to a crowd.

Kenny Victor, 57, sat on a couch in the back, looking a bit tearful. He said he was a Navy veteran and that he welcomed the decision. "I served for the right to vote," he said. "It's long overdue. We need representation."

Democrats, Don't Take Native American Voters for Granted

OPINION | BY TRISTAN AHTONE | OCT. 29, 2018

The party ignored voter suppression in Indian Country until a Senate seat in North Dakota was at risk.

AHEAD OF THE midterm elections, the state of North Dakota is using one of the most restrictive voter identification laws in the country to engage in that most American of traditions: excluding and discriminating against indigenous people.

Thanks to the state's Republican Party, all who want to take part in the democratic process must have a residential address on their identification cards. However, many tribal citizens in North Dakota don't have residential addresses or postal service. There are five federally recognized tribes in the state, with five reservations. More than 31,000 indigenous people live in North Dakota, and around 60 percent of that population lives on reservations. Those tribal citizens are usually issued tribal ID cards by their nations or by the Bureau of Indian Affairs. That makes those documents federally recognized, and once issued, they can be used for everything from getting through security at the airport to opening bank accounts. But they can no longer be used to vote.

This is egregious even by the standards of Republicans' all-out voter suppression war. Native voters in the state typically cast ballots for Democrats, and a quick glance at voting maps shows that they are concentrated in four areas — islands of blue in a sea of red. If those Democrat-leaning areas are overlaid on maps of the state's reservations, the boundaries align. With the new voter ID law, which will exclude voters in precisely these areas, those blue precincts can now turn red. Magic!

I have been covering elections in Indian Country since 2008, and while North Dakota's move isn't unusual, the stakes in this election feel higher. As the American empire begins its descent into Balkanization, Native voters could play a key role, and perhaps even slow the process, by voting for people who have represented their interests. In North Dakota, that person is Senator Heidi Heitkamp, a Democrat who was elected in 2012 with the help of Native voters.

Democrats are fuming over the disenfranchisement of Native voters now that a Senate seat is at stake, and reporters are descending on North Dakota to cover the problem. Yet there was little national attention in 2013 when the ID law was first introduced, in 2015 when it was made more restrictive by also banning college ID's, in 2016 when it was ruled unconstitutional or in 2017 when it was reintroduced and again ruled unconstitutional by a district court.

North Dakota Republicans have soldiered on: The state appealed the district court's ruling, the Court of Appeals for the Eighth Circuit overturned it, and on Oct. 9, the United States Supreme Court denied an application to stop the state from applying the law. When voters in North Dakota go to the polls on Nov. 6, they may find that the same ID they used to vote in the primary months earlier is no longer accepted.

It is a travesty of democracy, but for indigenous people in America, it is nothing new. We were not granted full citizenship until 1924, and in 1938, seven states still refused Native Americans the right to vote. Utah holds the honor of being the last state to enfranchise Native Americans, in 1957.

Democrats who say they care about Native American voting rights should acknowledge that these struggles continue. In 2014, the American Civil Liberties Union filed suit against San Juan County, in southeast Utah, after officials closed polling places and switched to mail-in ballots even though many Navajo don't have residential addresses or postal service. As recently as August, a federal judge had to intervene to put a Navajo candidate back onto the ballot for county commissioner after he was removed by San Juan County officials.

In 2016 in Nevada, the Pyramid Lake Paiutes and the Walker River Paiutes sued the state for denying tribal citizens access to polling places and registration sites within their territories. That same year, the Supreme Court allowed the state of Arizona to bar organizers from picking up and delivering ballots to election sites close to Native voters who had no access to mail or would otherwise have to drive hours to cast votes.

If Democrats do manage to retake control of the House or the Senate, they should stand up for indigenous communities outside of election cycles.

The Indian Child Welfare Act, for example, which tries to keep Indian families together, is under attack with the support of anti-Indian hate groups that hope to repeal it. Democrats could pass additional legislation to support the act.

The Trump administration has seized land from the Mashpee Wampanoag in Massachusetts. Congress should establish pathways to have those lands returned.

The Keystone XL Pipeline, which would run from Canada down through Montana, South Dakota and Nebraska, continues construction despite numerous lawsuits from tribal nations. Democrats should demand analysis on the potential impacts of spill as well as how the project affects the United States' trust obligations to tribal nations.

When Native Americans cast their ballots in the United States, they do so with the knowledge that this nation's democracy and its electoral system are made possible by genocide and land theft. Many of us nevertheless choose to vote, but it is grotesque that we must now also fight to reform that system to have the chance to fully participate in it.

Democrats have had many opportunities to be true allies to indigenous people. Instead, they have saved their anger for when it suited their needs.

TRISTAN AHTONE is associate editor for tribal affairs at High Country News and president of the Native American Journalists Association.

Many Texas Voters Whose Citizenship Was Questioned Are in Fact Citizens

BY LIAM STACK | JAN. 29, 2019

A CLAIM MADE last week by the Texas secretary of state — that 95,000 registered voters had a citizenship status that could not be determined — appeared to fall apart on Tuesday when local election officials said many of the people were known to be United States citizens.

Some registered to vote when they applied for a driver's license at the Texas Department of Public Safety, which requires them to prove citizenship status to state officials. Others registered at naturalization ceremonies, a data point to which state officials said they did not have access.

Election officials in Harris County, home to Houston, said they received 30,000 names — the largest single batch of potential noncitizen voters — from the secretary of state's office on Monday. By Tuesday afternoon, they had determined that roughly 400 of those names were duplicates and 60 percent so far of the others were United States citizens.

"We are not willing to conclude at this point that we know of anybody on this list who is not a United States citizen," Douglas Ray, special assistant attorney for Harris County, said. "We may determine that at a later time, and we are going to investigate that very carefully, but as you can tell by the numbers, so far things ain't looking good for this list," referring to the state's claim.

Local officials reported similar findings on Tuesday in Fort Bend County, outside of Houston; Travis County, home to the state capital, Austin; and Williamson County, outside of Austin. All said they had been instructed by the secretary of state's office on Tuesday to disregard the names of voters who registered at state public-safety offices.

On Tuesday, the office of David Whitley, who was appointed secretary of state in December by Gov. Greg Abbott, said in a statement that it was continuing to work with local officials "to assist them in verifying eligibility of Texas voters."

"This is to ensure that any registered voters who provided proof of citizenship at the time they registered to vote will not be required to provide proof of citizenship as part of the counties' examination," the statement said.

In an announcement last Friday, Mr. Whitley's office questioned the citizenship status of 95,000 voters. That finding grew out of an 11-month investigation by the secretary of state's office and the Texas Department of Public Safety, which declined to comment on Tuesday.

Attorney General Ken Paxton, a Republican who has zealously prosecuted individual cases of voter fraud, quickly amplified that announcement with a pledge to investigate the names on the list. A spokeswoman for his office did not respond to a request for comment on Tuesday.

Democrats and voting-rights advocates expressed skepticism about the state's claims last week, pointing to the possibility of administrative error as well as the state's history of voter suppression.

Voter registration in many Texas counties is handled by the tax assessor, a holdover from the Jim Crow practice of collecting a poll tax, Mr. Ray said. Poll taxes were abolished by the 24th Amendment to the United States Constitution in 1964.

Kristen Clarke, the president of the Lawyers' Committee for Civil Rights Under Law, called the problems that arose on Tuesday "an unsurprising development." She said Mr. Paxton had been "reckless and irresponsible to race forward with broad, sweeping allegations without conducting full, due diligence."

Another group, the League of United Latin American Citizens, filed a federal lawsuit on Tuesday that accused Mr. Paxton and Mr. Whitley of violating the federal Voting Rights Act.

Mr. Davis, in Williamson County, said his office received a list of 2,067 names this week, including 34 duplicates. It began a "very methodical and very deliberate and careful" investigation into the remaining names and found many whose citizenship was not in question.

"We found some records where two things existed at once," Mr. Davis said. "One was the D.P.S. had identified them as potential non-citizens, but also these same people had registered to vote at the D.P.S. and so had been verified to be citizens."

Compounding problems for local officials is the fact that the so-called list is not actually a list.

John Oldham, the elections administrator in Fort Bend County, said four of his employees were combing through documents related to 8,035 people that his office received on Monday.

In Travis County, Bruce Elfant, the tax assessor-collector and voter registrar, said his office was trying to organize the "jumble" of information it received on 4,500 voters into a usable format. He said that even a cursory review of the information they received turned up a "significant" number of people who the secretary of state has now told them to remove.

"I said to the secretary of state's office this morning, 'It would have been nice if you sent it in a spreadsheet,' " he said. "They told me, 'Well, we didn't.' A lot of things would have been nice, I guess."

Florida Limits Ex-Felon Voting, Prompting a Lawsuit and Cries of 'Poll Tax'

BY PATRICIA MAZZEI | JUNE 28, 2019

MIAMI — Gov. Ron DeSantis of Florida signed into law on Friday significant restrictions to the recently restored voting rights of people with felony convictions, prompting the American Civil Liberties Union to sue the state hours later.

The new law requires people with serious criminal histories to fully pay back fines and fees to the courts before they become eligible to vote. In some cases, those costs amount to thousands of dollars.

The A.C.L.U. argued that the new limits would unconstitutionally price some people out of the ballot box and undermine the intent of Florida voters, who last November approved a measure to enfranchise up to 1.5 million former felons.

"There's no rational basis for treating somebody who can afford to pay fees any differently than treating anybody who can't afford to pay them," said Julie Ebenstein, a senior staff attorney with the A.C.L.U.'s Voting Rights Project. "That's just distinguishing people's right to vote based on their wealth."

Nearly 65 percent of Florida voters backed the measure to enfranchise ex-felons, Amendment 4, which many felt could reshape the electorate of the nation's largest presidential battleground state. African-Americans, who tend to vote Democratic, have been disproportionately disenfranchised, though the majority of those with felony convictions in Florida are white.

State lawmakers in the Republican-controlled Legislature said they were not motivated by politics when they adopted restrictions to Amendment 4 last month. Instead, they said they needed to clarify how the measure would be put into practice. The text of the amendment

Voters registering at the Miami-Dade County Elections office on Jan. 8, the day a measure restoring voting rights to ex-felons went into effect. Under a new law, former felons will have to pay off fines and court fees before registering to vote.

itself, they argued, required a strict interpretation of what constitutes the completion of a felony sentence — which includes repaying financial obligations, sometimes tens of thousands of dollars, to the courts.

Mr. DeSantis's office did not issue a statement explaining his decision to sign the bill. But he had promised to do so, and faced a Saturday deadline.

"The controversy, to me, is not really substantive," Mr. DeSantis told a Miami news station last week. "The people who advocated for this, I mean, they went to the Supreme Court, and they said, 'Of course, whatever you're sentenced to, you have to finish — whether that's incarceration, whether that's a fine, restitution, probation.' "

Still, the timing of the governor's action, announced after 6 p.m. on a Friday, seemed intended to draw little attention from Florida voters, more of whom voted for Amendment 4 than for him. Not long afterward, the A.C.L.U. filed its lawsuit in Federal District Court for the Northern District of Florida, joined by the A.C.L.U. of Florida, the N.A.A.C.P. Legal Defense and Educational Fund and the Brennan Center for Justice at New York University.

Groups that helped pass Amendment 4 have continued to hold registration drives, trying to add as many ex-felons to the rolls as possible before the new restrictions become effective on Monday. Under Amendment 4, people with felony convictions had been eligible to register as of January. Some of them have already cast ballots in local elections.

Among them was Jeff Gruver, 33, one of the plaintiffs in the A.C.L.U. lawsuit. Mr. Gruver, who runs a homeless shelter in Gainesville, Fla., was so eager to vote for the first time in his life that he tried registering right after Election Day in November, only to be rejected because the amendment was not in effect yet. He voted in a mayoral election earlier this year.

"I was so, so excited," he said. "I went to the polling place, which is right next to my house. I got my I.D. out and, and I even showed them my registration card. I was like, 'Look at this!' and they said, 'You don't need to show that.' I said, 'No, you don't understand.' "

Mr. Gruver spent about 10 months over several stints in jail for cocaine possession and for violating the terms of his probation. He was addicted to heroin and opiates for about a decade before joining Narcotics Anonymous and getting clean, he said.

Mr. Gruver was assessed $801 in court costs in 2008. He said he cannot afford to make a payment like that.

"I have paid for what I've done in more ways than one," he said.

Another plaintiff, Betty Riddle, who works as a communications assistant at the public defender's office in Sarasota, Fla., regained her voting rights at 61. She completed her prison sentence in 2002 and now deals with others caught in the criminal justice system.

"I was in hog heaven," she said. "I thought I would never vote."

She still owes more than $1,000 in court costs and fees, which she said she cannot afford to pay.

"I don't think it's fair," she said. "It is a poll tax to keep us from voting."

Kentucky Gives Voting Rights to Some 140,000 Former Felons

BY MICHAEL WINES | DEC. 12, 2019

The state's new Democratic governor said he would ease one of the nation's strictest policies. Iowa will be alone in barring voting by all felons.

KENTUCKY'S NEWLY ELECTED Democratic governor, Andy Beshear, signed an executive order on Thursday restoring the vote and the right to hold public office to more than 140,000 residents who have completed sentences for nonviolent felonies.

With that move, Kentucky joined a fast-growing movement to return voting rights to former felons, leaving Iowa as the only state that strips all former felons of the right to cast a ballot.

Since 1997, 24 states have approved some type of measure to ease voting bans, according to the Sentencing Project, a Washington group that advocates criminal justice policy changes. Kentucky joins Virginia, Florida, Nevada and other states that have extended voting rights in the last few years.

Mr. Beshear said the order would apply to more than half of the estimated 240,000 Kentuckians with felonies in their past, as well as those who complete their sentences in the future.

While he believes in justice, he said, "I also believe in second chances."

"We're talking about moms and dads, neighbors and friends, people who have met and taken on one of the greatest challenges anyone can face: overcoming the past," the governor said. "It is an injustice that their ability to rejoin society by casting a vote on Election Day is automatically denied."

Voting-rights advocates called Kentucky's decision a significant advance in a campaign to return the vote to felons that began decades ago and has won widespread attention and support only recently.

But while the most recent changes have returned voting rights to well over 1.5 million people nationwide, it remains unclear how they will affect the political process. A handful of academic studies suggest that former prisoners register and vote at rates well below national averages.

The governor said his order did not extend to those who committed violent felonies because some offenses, such as rape and murder, were too heinous to forgive. The order also excludes those who were convicted under federal law or the laws of other states, although they would be able to apply individually for restoration of their rights.

Notably, the order does not require former felons to complete payment of fines or other legal costs before winning the right to vote, an issue that has snarled implementation of a 2018 ballot initiative that ordered the restoration of voting rights in Florida.

Kentucky's Constitution denies the vote to anyone with a felony conviction but allows the governor to restore that right to individuals. In remarks at the State Capitol, Mr. Beshear urged the Legislature to remove that ban through an amendment, but said that he would seek to make the restoration process as automatic as possible until that occurred.

"Our goal is that no one will have to fill out a form," he said. "And our goal is to create a system and a process where any of these individuals now living in all parts of Kentucky can go into any clerk's office" and register to vote without difficulty.

"I hope today is just the start of righting a lot of injustices," he said.

The order signed on Thursday in effect revives a similar order that the governor's father, Steve Beshear, himself a former governor, signed in his last days in office in 2015. His Republican successor, Matt Bevin, revoked it.

Andy Beshear ended Mr. Bevin's re-election bid last month, winning the race for governor by barely 5,000 votes. Mr. Bevin, who was widely unpopular even among Republicans, at first claimed the election was marred by irregularities, then said he had lost because Democrats were "so good at harvesting votes in urban communities."

In Iowa, now the only state with a total ban on voting by former felons, a Democratic governor also signed an order restoring rights to some former felons. But the measure, enacted in 2005, was revoked by his Republican successor. The current Republican governor, Kim Reynolds, has supported re-enfranchising former felons, but the State Legislature has not acted on the matter.

Mr. Beshear's order won quick praise from civil rights and criminal justice organizations, even as they expressed disappointment that it covered only some citizens who have been returned to society.

"This is a giant step forward, and I think the momentum gained by making Iowa the only one left is really going to fast-track normalizing this issue," said Myrna Pérez, the director of the voting rights and elections program at the Brennan Center for Justice at New York University. "The fewer states you have with permanent disenfranchisement, the easier it is to move the baseline."

The issue has long been a flashpoint for civil rights groups. But the movement made national headlines only in 2016, when Virginia's Democratic governor at the time, Terry McAuliffe, signed an order giving voting rights to some 156,000 former felons.

Like Kentucky, Virginia bars felons from voting for life unless a governor restores their right, a decades-old restriction that, like similar measures in some other states, was designed at least in part to disenfranchise African-Americans. The state had gradually lowered the barriers to winning restoration, but Mr. McAuliffe effectively removed all obstacles and made restoration automatic for those who had completed their sentences.

The movement gained further steam in 2018, when Florida voters approved a constitutional amendment restoring voting rights to roughly 1.4 million former felons, excepting those convicted of murder or sex offenses.

Since then, Nevada has removed a ban on voting for 77,000 citizens on parole or probation, Louisiana has eased a ban affecting about 40,000 former felons under supervision, and New Jersey's Legislature appears poised to pass similar legislation. Colorado has extended the vote to parolees and required its corrections department to notify them of their rights, and Arizona has abolished a requirement that first-time felons pay outstanding fines to win back their voting rights.

There has been some pushback. Some experts say the restoration of voting rights in Kentucky and Florida was limited in scope because public support was weak for giving the vote to people who had committed violent crimes, even if they had completed their sentences.

In Florida, Republicans blunted the impact of the voter-approved amendment by passing a law that required former felons to pay all fines, restitution and court costs before being deemed to have completed their sentences. The measure effectively denied the vote to hundreds of thousands of those who are too poor to pay the fees or are paying them in installments that will not be completed for years.

Florida's Supreme Court is considering a challenge to the law and is expected to issue a ruling early next year.

Many analysts say Republican opposition to restoring voting rights is at least partly rooted in politics because a disproportionate number of former felons are members of minority groups that tend to vote for Democrats. But some of the few studies on the issue suggest that political concerns may be exaggerated, or even outright wrong.

One recent analysis, a 2015 review of Iowa's brief restoration of the vote to ex-felons, found that only about 15 percent of recently enfranchised people cast ballots in the 2008 presidential election. A 2009 study of 666 former felons in Erie County, N.Y., concluded that their turnout was in the single-digit range. And the researchers who conducted the Iowa study have cited statistics indicating that former felons tend to register as Democrats in some states and as independents in others.

Voting-rights advocates allowed that participation appears low but say that is a diversion from their central premise: that people should not be denied the right to vote as punishment for a criminal record.

That view appears to have gained public support as tough-on-crime laws and drug epidemics like the current opioid crisis have expanded the so-called criminal class to wide segments of mainstream society. In Kentucky, nearly one in 10 white people has a felony record, often because of comparatively low-level narcotics violations. For African-Americans, the consequences are far greater; one in four — and one in three men — has a felony record.

In any case, advocates said, there is ample reason to believe that the voting record of newly released prisoners has nowhere to go but up. The Iowa study included, for example, that participation grew when former felons were educated about their new voting rights, removing confusion about whether casting a ballot still violated the law.

"It'll be interesting to see what happens in Kentucky," said Marc Mauer, the executive director of the Sentencing Project. "It's one thing for the governor to sign a paper saying they have the right to vote, but how does that work? Does everyone get a piece of paper in the mail? Does anyone describe to you how to register to vote?"

And Ms. Pérez, from the Brennan Center, said she believed low turnout among former felons was but "the tip of the iceberg."

"They're trying to get jobs, trying to maintain sobriety, trying to get their children back. Voting is just one of the important things they're trying to do," she said. "This is going to need some time to ramp up, and it will need people to speak out loud that they matter. These people are starting out so far behind because they've gotten the message for so long that they don't count."

MICHAEL WINES writes about voting and other election-related issues. Since joining The Times in 1988, he has covered the Justice Department, the White House, Congress, Russia, southern Africa, China and various other topics.

CHAPTER 2

The Impact of Voter Fraud and ID Laws

Strict voter ID laws — enacted by state governments with the stated goal of preventing voter fraud — have been one of the more common methods of voter suppression. In 2017, President Trump launched a short-lived commission on voter fraud, which was disbanded after election officials from both Republican and Democratic areas refused to supply personal data about their voters. State policies were challenged in court with varying results: A Texas law was upheld in 2018, while a North Carolina law was struck down in 2017 for targeting African-Americans.

Why Voter ID Laws Don't Swing Many Elections

ANALYSIS | BY NATE COHN | NOV. 19, 2014

MANY PEOPLE HAVE understandably blamed low turnout for the Democratic Party's misfortune on Nov. 4, but some have gone a step further.

They argue that turnout was so low because of voter suppression, particularly laws requiring voters to present photo identification. They assert that these laws disenfranchised enough voters to decide several elections, even a Kansas governor's contest where a Republican won by four percentage points.

Voter ID laws might well be a cynical, anti-democratic attempt to disenfranchise voters to help Republicans, as Democrats claim. But that doesn't mean that voter ID laws are an effective way to steal elections. They just don't make a difference in anything but the closest contests, when anything and everything matters.

This may come as a surprise to those who have read articles hyperventilating about the laws. Dave Weigel at Slate in 2012 said a Pennsylvania voter identification law might disenfranchise 759,000 registered voters, a possibility he described as "an apocalypse." Pennsylvania's voter ID law was reversed before the election, but it is not hard to see why so many thought it could be decisive when Mr. Obama won the state with a 309,840 vote margin.

But the so-called margin of disenfranchisement — the number of registered voters who do not appear to have photo identification — grossly overstates the potential electoral consequences of these laws.

These figures overstate the number of voters who truly lack identification. Those without ID are particularly unlikely to vote. And many who do vote will vote Republican. In the end, the seemingly vast registration gaps dwindle, leaving enough voters to decide only elections determined by fractions of a point.

To begin with, the true number of registered voters without photo identification is usually much lower than the statistics on registered voters without identification suggest. The number of voters without photo identification is calculated by matching voter registration files with state ID databases. But perfect matching is impossible, and the effect is to overestimate the number of voters without identification.

Take Texas, a state with a particularly onerous voter ID law. If I register to vote as "Nate" but my ID says "Nathan," I might be counted among the hundreds of thousands of registered voters without a photo ID. But I'll be fine at the polling station on Election Day with a name that's "substantially similar" to the one on file.

The matching issues run well beyond substantive ones like nicknames. If you've ever worked with voter files, you know that they're rife with minor errors — like a first name in the middle name column —

that prevent exact matching. The scale of the matching problem was highlighted in a North Carolina Board of Elections study last year. The state used a long list of matching criteria, ranging from names and Social Security numbers and date of birth to a "soundex" comparison to test for names that were entered slightly off but sound the same. After additional matching criteria, the number of unmatched registered voters plummeted from 1.24 million to 318,643.

Even that figure likely overstates the number of registered voters without a valid identification, since many voters have valid identifications that aren't issued by the states. Passports, student IDs and military IDs are often allowed.

I do not have a Washington, D.C., identification, just a Washington State driver's license and a United States passport. I would be grouped among the voters without a photo identification in a D.C. study, but I would be able to vote using my passport in an actual election. It is hard to say just how many people there are like me, but it probably isn't an irrelevant number: There are 117 million valid passports in circulation, or enough for about 37 percent of Americans.

People without ID are less likely to vote than other registered voters. The North Carolina study found that 43 percent of the unmatched voters — registered voters who could not be matched with a driver's license — participated in 2012, compared with more than 70 percent of matched voters.

It shouldn't be surprising that more of the unmatched voters stayed home. The demographic profile of voters without identification — young, nonwhite, poor, immobile, elderly — is also similar to the profile of voters who turn out at low rates. It's also possible that the voter file is the issue. Some people voted in past elections, but have moved since and haven't been purged from the voter file, even though their ID may have expired (if they had one in the first place). Some elderly voters might just be dead and not yet removed from the voter rolls.

It certainly is not clear that those without a photo ID would overwhelmingly support Democrats. There's no question that voter ID has a disparate impact on Democratic-leaning groups — those young, non-white, poor, immobile or elderly voters. The unmatched North Carolina voters were registered as Democrats by a 37-point margin, compared with the 12-point Democratic margin statewide. They were 46 percent nonwhite, compared with 29 percent of all registered voters.

But 22 percent of these voters were registered Republicans. The voters without an identification might be breaking something more like 70/30 for Democrats than 95/5.

A 70/30 margin is a big deal, and, again, it's fully consistent with Democratic concerns about voter suppression. But when we're down to the subset of unmatched voters who don't have any identification and still vote, a 70/30 margin probably isn't generating enough votes to decide anything but an extremely close election.

Finally, many of the voters without valid identification will cast provisional ballots. The provisional ballot process is not an adequate remedy for voters without an identification; many voters without identification will be dissuaded from voting. Nonetheless, 37 percent of provisional ballots cast because of ID reasons were counted in Kansas and 26 percent were counted in Tennessee in 2012, according to a Government Accountability Office analysis.

When all of these mitigating factors come into play, the case for voter ID laws swinging anything but the closest election gets very shaky. The studies ostensibly showing a relationship between voter ID and Republican strength are dubious, at best. They often conflate changes in turnout resulting from other factors, like whether there's a statewide election, with changes caused by voter ID laws.

The impact of voter ID laws is basically indiscernible in the results. Democrats have pulled off impressive wins in states with voter ID, including perhaps the single most impressive electoral feat of the last decade: President Obama's victory in Indiana in 2008, which came just after the state passed a voter ID law.

Voter disenfranchisement is anti-democratic, regardless of whether it swings elections. But voter ID laws haven't been swinging elections.

Maine Republicans Want to Get There (Vote Suppression) From Here (Vote Turnout)

OPINION | BY ANDREW ROSENTHAL | NOV. 15, 2011

EARLIER THIS YEAR, Maine's governor, Paul LePage, a Tea Party favorite, helped Republican legislators enact a law eliminating Maine's 38-year-old same-day voter registration policy. They offered the standard excuse Republicans have been using around the country to hinder turnout by Democratic-leaning groups — it was necessary to prevent voter fraud.

Never mind that voter fraud — people trying to vote when they are not entitled to — is no bigger a problem in Maine than in the rest of the country, which is to say it's not much of a problem at all. Maine has reported two cases in 38 years.

Last week, a resounding 60 percent of Maine's voters nullified that law, but that hasn't stopped Republicans in the state house from seeking new ways to combat an imaginary crisis. Now they're pushing a bill that would require voters to show photo identification at the polls.

The GOP has already imposed voter ID laws on seven states and introduced them in more than 25 others. In each case the intent, or at least the effect, is the same: Voter suppression, mostly of the elderly and minority groups.

Every time I write about voter ID laws, I get a flood of angry messages over email and Twitter, and confused comments on this blog, many from readers who genuinely don't understand why this is a big deal. So I thought I'd try to clear things up.

The last time I addressed voter fraud, for instance, some asked why it is OK to require a photo ID to get on an airplane, or buy liquor, or food stamps, but not to vote.

Buying liquor is not a constitutional right, nor is getting on a particular plane. Getting food stamps is a privilege, not a right, and fraud in this area has been very well documented. In our insecure world, requiring ID to enter a federal building is a reasonable precaution. Requiring one to vote is not, especially since IDs represent an undue burden on certain groups.

But *why is it a burden*, you ask? As one reader explained, government-issued photo IDs usually cost something, so they could be considered a poll tax.

Even if states were to offer official photo IDs for free (and some do already), would-be voters would still need to take time off from work, and travel, to get their applications processed. And, remember, people without photo IDs don't have driver's licenses, and probably don't have a car. Moreover, as another reader noted, we live in a mobile society and ID addresses don't keep up with our movements. Many Americans do not have a permanent address at all.

Getting an ID necessitates strong English and an understanding of bureaucracies, neither of which are requirements to vote. And it means knowing that the rules exit. Many people will turn up at the polls without an ID and get turned away. All of these problems are toughest on poor people, alienated minority groups and people in rural areas.

For some Americans, especially African-Americans, there is also history. Governments in this country have tried all kinds of ways, including intimidation, bureaucratic rules, poll taxes and outright violence to keep them away from the polls. A law requiring a photo ID could be seen by minorities as just another way of keep them from casting their votes.

My bottom line is this: There is no justifying a requirement that falls hardest on poor people and minorities. Voting is the ultimate expression of American democracy. The more people that vote in an election, the more democratic it is.

ANDREW ROSENTHAL is the Editorial Page editor of The Times, overseeing the newspaper's Opinion section.

The Republicans' Obsession With Voter Suppression

OPINION | BY FRANCIS X. CLINES | MAY 20, 2016

A FEDERAL COURT JUDGE has struck down an outrageous attempt by Kansas Republicans to force potential voters into a labyrinthine registration process of documenting their citizenship with birth certificates, passports or naturalization papers. This blatantly anti-democratic law, enacted in 2013 by Kansas lawmakers, had side-tracked 18,000 citizens onto an official "in suspense" list earlier this year, leaving them unregistered and unable to vote in federal elections until investigators pored through their documentation.

The transparent scheme of voter suppression was found in violation of federal law by Judge Julie Robinson in Kansas City who pointed to "the risk of thousands of otherwise eligible voters being disenfranchised in upcoming federal elections." Last Tuesday, the judge ordered state officials to begin fully registering the suspended applicants on June 1, without the burden of producing a birth certificate or other papers.

Federal law allows people to register when they get a driver's license or state ID and attest under criminal threat of perjury that they are who they say they are. Republicans intent on holding down the votes of minorities and young people have been adding roadblocks through draconian state laws. In suing Kansas, the American Civil Liberties Union pointed out that more than 58 percent of the people on the Kansas "suspense" list were citizens aged 18 to 29, presumably excited by this year's campaigns but denied their normal voter registration rights.

Republicans pushed the law on the claim that voter fraud is rampant in the country. Various studies have proven this untrue. The scheme was driven by the Kansas secretary of state, Kris Kobach, who was given extraordinary powers last year to prosecute voter fraud.

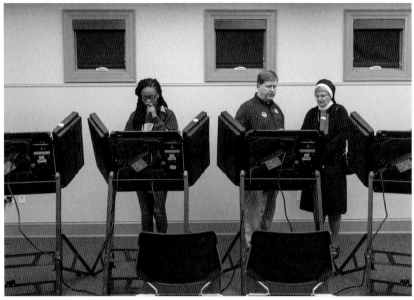

Voters cast their ballots in the 2016 Missouri primary.

But he's achieved just one conviction so far, thereby demonstrating the rarity of voter fraud. One of his Kansas political allies, Brian Newby, has used his new position as executive director of the United States Election Assistance Commission to attempt to bypass commission members and unilaterally decree that Kansas can alter the federal voter registration form and mandate extra documentation.

Republicans' obsession with voter suppression also continues fiercely in Missouri, where a decade ago state courts struck down a law mandating that voters show up with photo identification in order to cast a ballot. The Republican state legislature remains undaunted, approving a referendum this year in which voters will be asked to approve a constitutional amendment requiring that they henceforth show photo IDs at the ballot box.

FRANCIS X. CLINES is a member of the editorial board.

Some Republicans Acknowledge Leveraging Voter ID Laws for Political Gain

BY MICHAEL WINES | SEPT. 16, 2016

AS ONE PROMINENT and much beloved Republican once said — actually, repeatedly said — "There you go again."

Deep in a trove of leaked documents made public this week was the latest example of Republican candor over voter ID laws — this time in Wisconsin.

There, as a tight race for election to the state's Supreme Court came to a close in April 2011, conservative leaders wondered aloud how to respond should Justice David Prosser Jr. — a reliable opponent of legal challenges to the agenda of Gov. Scott Walker, a Republican — go down in defeat.

A senior vice president of the Metropolitan Milwaukee Chamber of Commerce, Steve Baas, had a thought. "Do we need to start messaging 'widespread reports of election fraud' so we are positively set up for the recount regardless of the final number?" he wrote in an email on April 6 to conservative strategists. "I obviously think we should."

Scott Jensen, a Republican political tactician and former speaker of the State Assembly, responded within minutes. "Yes. Anything fishy should be highlighted," he wrote. "Stories should be solicited by talk radio hosts."

That email exchange, part of documents published by The Guardian on Wednesday with a report on Governor Walker's political operations, was followed by a spate of public rumors of vote-rigging. A month later, legislators passed a state law requiring Wisconsin voters to display one of five types of approved photo IDs before casting ballots.

The Wisconsin statute was part of a wave of voter ID laws enacted in the last six years, mostly by Republican-controlled legislatures whose leaders claimed that cheating at the ballot box is a routine occurrence.

Yet academic studies and election-law experts broadly agree that voter fraud is not a widespread problem in American elections. Rather, they say, it is a widespread political tactic used either to create doubt about an election's validity or to keep one's opponents — in most cases, Democratic voters — from casting ballots.

In unguarded moments, some Republican supporters of the laws have been inclined to agree.

CLAIMING DEMOCRATIC VOTERS CHEAT

In April of this year, Representative Glenn Grothman, Republican of Wisconsin, predicted in a television interview that the state's photo ID law would weaken the Democratic presidential candidate Hillary Clinton's chances of winning the state in November's election.

It was not the first time he cited voter ID requirements' impact on Democrats; in 2012, speaking about the law's effect on President Obama's re-election race, Mr. Grothman said voter ID requirements hurt Democrats because Democratic voters cheat more often — a premise that remains unproven. One of the few verified instances of recent voter fraud at a Wisconsin polling place — the only kind of fraud that a photo ID might prevent — padded a Republican governor's tally.

'HAPPY' TO DENY THE RIGHT TO VOTE

Also in Wisconsin, Todd Allbaugh, 46, a staff aide to a Republican state legislator, attributed his decision to quit his job in 2015 and leave the party to what he witnessed at a Republican caucus meeting. He wrote on Facebook:

I was in the closed Senate Republican Caucus when the final round of multiple Voter ID bills were being discussed. A handful of the GOP Senators were giddy about the ramifications and literally singled out the prospects of suppressing minority and college voters. Think about that for a minute. Elected officials planning and happy to help deny a fellow American's constitutional right to vote in order to increase their own chances to hang onto power.

LOWERING DEMOCRATS' MARGINS OF VICTORY

In Pennsylvania, the state Republican Party chairman, Robert Gleason, told an interviewer that the state's voter ID law "had helped a bit" in lowering President Obama's margin of victory over the Republican presidential nominee Mitt Romney in the state in 2012.

HELPING REPUBLICANS IN SWING STATES

In that same election, the Republican leader of the Pennsylvania House of Representatives, Mike Turzai, predicted during the campaign that the voter ID law would "allow Governor Romney to win the state of Pennsylvania, done."

PART OF THE PARTY'S TOOL KIT

And also that year, Scott Tranter, a Republican political consultant for Mr. Romney and others, called voter ID laws — and generating long lines at polling places — part of his party's tool kit.

PARTISAN GAINS

Don Yelton, a North Carolina Republican Party county precinct chairman, told an interviewer for Comedy Central's "The Daily Show" in 2013 that the state's voter ID law would "kick the Democrats in the butt." Mr. Yelton later resigned; the party disavowed his statements.

A 'MARKETING PLOY'

In Florida, both the state's former Republican Party chairman, Jim Greer, and its former Republican governor, Charlie Crist, told The Palm Beach Post in 2012 that the state's voter ID law was devised to suppress Democratic votes. Mr. Greer told The Post: "The Republican Party, the strategists, the consultants, they firmly believe that early voting is bad for Republican Party candidates. It's done for one reason and one reason only," he said. Consultants told him "we've got to cut down on early voting because early voting is not good for us," he said.

He added, "They never came in to see me and tell me we had a fraud issue. It's all a marketing ploy."

As for Wisconsin's law, two federal courts ruled this summer that the ID requirement disenfranchised citizens who had trouble obtaining an approved ID card — many of them minorities who vote Democratic. While the legal battle continues, the state has been ordered to offer an easier way to obtain identification.

Similar laws in North Carolina and Texas were struck down this summer by federal courts that called them racially discriminatory. A federal appeals court ruling in the North Carolina case concluded that that state's election law had targeted African-American voters because they were overwhelmingly Democrats.

Of course, no voting system is foolproof. Early this month, a St. Louis judge ordered a new Democratic primary election in Missouri's 78th State House District. The losing candidate in the August election, Bruce Franks, cited irregularities in the city election board's handling of absentee ballots.

But such incidents are isolated. And virtually all of them, including the allegations in the St. Louis case, involve schemes like manipulating absentee ballots or falsifying returns that voter ID laws could not detect, much less prevent.

The only fraud that such laws might stop — misrepresentation at a polling place to cast an illegal ballot — is vanishingly rare. And for good reason: To swing most elections, dozens or hundreds of fraudsters would have to conspire to commit easily detected felonies at polling places on behalf of their favored candidate.

Richard L. Hasen, an election law expert and law professor at the University of California, Irvine, said in an email on Thursday that spreading claims of voter fraud for political gain has a pernicious impact.

"It is a shameful falsehood, given the extremely low rates of voter fraud in the U.S., especially the kind of fraud targeted by Republican voter ID laws," he wrote. "It undermines faith in the fairness of the electoral process, which is the bedrock of all functioning democracies."

Yet it is now approaching conventional wisdom: In a new poll, nearly half of Americans said they believe voter fraud happens somewhat or very often in elections.

Questions and
Answers on Voter Fraud

BY ALAN BLINDER | AUG. 4, 2016

WHEN DONALD J. TRUMP suggested this week that recent court rulings against voter identification laws could contribute to a "rigged" election this fall, his comments ran counter to the findings of many judges and researchers, who say such statutes aim at a form of fraud that is rare and typically isolated.

Mr. Trump's remarks, which he made during an interview with The Washington Post, align closely with arguments long advanced by supporters of voter identification laws, including Republican governors and state legislators.

"We may have people vote 10 times," Mr. Trump told The Post. "It's inconceivable that you don't have to show identification in order to vote or that the identification doesn't have to be somewhat foolproof."

He said later, "If you don't have voter ID, you can just keep voting and voting and voting."

Here are some questions and answers about election fraud.

WHAT TYPES OF FRAUD HAPPEN?

While supporters of voter identification laws say they worry about acts of impersonation at polling places, the federal and state authorities have brought some cases involving other types of misconduct. In some instances, immigrants cast ballots when they were not eligible to do so. In others, convicted felons voted, even though they were barred from doing so. Other people have been accused of submitting multiple ballots, or of using illegitimate addresses to register to vote.

Investigators say that in many cases of election fraud, cluelessness, not criminality, is to blame.

"Occasionally, we may come up with a piece of information that someone has registered to vote and, in fact, he or she does not qualify," said James I. Cabezas, the chief investigator for the Maryland State Prosecutor's Office, which opened in 1977 to examine allegations of political corruption. "But in those cases, 99 percent, it's innocent error. They think they're eligible, but they're not."

Mr. Cabezas, who has been with the office since its inception, recalled one case.

"She had a green card," Mr. Cabezas recounted, "and she said, 'I knew I wasn't a U.S. citizen, but I took a U.S. history course, and the history teacher told me I could vote.' "

HOW COMMON IS IN-PERSON VOTER FRAUD?

Such fraud happens, but is rare, and reports of misconduct are often overstated in the press and on social media.

The Government Accountability Office, in a report last year, acknowledged the challenge of making "a complete estimate of the incidence of in-person voter fraud," but its review of five studies "identified few instances of in-person voter fraud."

There are few prosecutions for any type of election fraud, even in a country where, in 2000, more than 105 million people voted for a presidential candidate. During the administration of President George W. Bush, the Justice Department pursued what was widely regarded as a crackdown on voter fraud. In the first five years, about 120 people were charged and 86 convicted.

News21, a reporting project affiliated with Arizona State University, found in 2012 that there had been 2,068 cases of fraud nationwide since 2000, including episodes of absentee ballot fraud, intimidation, vote-buying and double voting. In at least a quarter of the investigations, the authorities did not bring charges.

Ten of the cases reviewed by News21 involved voter impersonation, and most of those investigations led to plea agreements or guilty verdicts at trial.

DO VOTER ID LAWS PREVENT IN-PERSON FRAUD?

According to their supporters, yes. But a federal appeals court was skeptical as recently as last week that North Carolina's voter identification law would stop fraud, particularly because it did not do anything to prevent fraud that might happen through absentee voting.

The law, a three-judge panel of the United States Court of Appeals for the Fourth Circuit concluded, was "not restrictive enough to effectively prevent voter fraud."

Researchers who have evaluated many identification laws also question their efficacy at preventing in-person fraud.

"My research confirms that there are hundreds of reports of alleged fraud, in thousands of elections, with millions of ballots cast," Justin Levitt, a law professor at Loyola University in Los Angeles, wrote in a 2012 paper.

But, Professor Levitt said, removing "unreliable and irrelevant reports" of fraud left "only a handful of reports that even allege, much less substantiate, instances of fraud that increased identification requirements at the polls could prevent."

SO COULD FRAUD DECIDE A NATIONAL ELECTION?

Almost certainly not, chiefly because the enforcement of voter ID laws would guard solely against in-person fraud, which has been strikingly rare. Experts also say that the risk of widespread, decisive misconduct in a national election is extremely slim, in part because of the number of regulators from both parties and the constitutional structure of presidential balloting.

But there is bipartisan agreement that, under exceptional circumstances, fraud could taint contests involving far fewer votes, like some local races.

MICHAEL WINES contributed reporting.

Donald Trump Campaign Seeks 'Voter Suppression,' Report Says, but It's Legal

BY MAGGIE HABERMAN AND JEREMY W. PETERS | OCT. 27, 2016

DONALD J. TRUMP'S CAMPAIGN set off a wave of concern about its tactics on Thursday after a senior campaign official was quoted describing a sophisticated "voter suppression" effort, a term that usually connotes aggressive attempts to keep people from polling places.

The anxiety among Republicans outside the Trump campaign was set off by a report in Businessweek in which the unidentified official used the term to describe the team's approach to three core groups of Hillary Clinton's supporters.

The report came after weeks of diatribes from Mr. Trump questioning the basic integrity of the election. At a rally on Thursday afternoon, he joked that the election should be called off and he should be crowned the winner.

" 'We have three major voter suppression operations underway,' says a senior official," the Businessweek report said. "They're aimed at three groups Clinton needs to win overwhelmingly: idealistic white liberals, young women, and African-Americans."

"Voter suppression" often refers to activities, legal and illegal, aimed at preventing eligible voters from casting ballots, such as by passing out fliers containing the wrong date for an election.

But the Businessweek report went on to explain tactics that are more aptly described as efforts aimed at depressing a rival's turnout, such as informing black voters of Mrs. Clinton's comment in 1994, while her husband pushed for a bill to reduce urban crime, describing some black teenagers as "superpredators."

The report contained no examples of the more aggressive efforts that the phrase "voter suppression" usually describes.

STEPHEN CROWLEY/THE NEW YORK TIMES

Donald J. Trump on Thursday in Toledo, Ohio. A report quoted a top campaign official describing a "voter suppression" effort, but it did not specify any illegal or aggressive tactics.

"What it appears the quote is describing is an attempt to discourage certain demographic groups from turning out in large numbers," said Jason Torchinsky, a Republican election lawyer.

"For lawyers and judges," Mr. Torchinsky said, "these terms usually invoke memories of actions such as placing armed individuals outside polling places or sending letters telling legal voters that if they vote, they will go to jail."

Jason Miller, a spokesman for Mr. Trump, insisted that the Businessweek report did not accurately reflect the campaign's approach. "Whoever described it as such either a) doesn't know what they're talking about or b) just isn't dialed in to our campaign and what Mr. Trump is trying to accomplish," he said.

Mr. Trump's own language about the election has raised concerns among Democrats and some Republican election lawyers. He has repeatedly said that there was evidence that the outcome would be "rigged" and has urged his supporters to monitor urban polling places after they vote, a suggestion that some say could lead his followers to enter the sites illegally and intimidate minority voters.

His language prompted the Democratic National Committee to file court papers this week asking to extend a decades-old consent decree barring the Republican National Committee from using tactics that could prevent people from voting. The Trump campaign is not bound by that consent decree, but his team works in tandem with the party committee.

Aides to Mrs. Clinton and an official with the Democratic National Committee did not respond to requests for comment about the Trump team's remarks. A spokesman for the Justice Department declined to comment.

It is highly unusual for a campaign official to boast of using "voter suppression." Still, there is little indication that the Trump campaign is doing anything more sophisticated or aggressive than using legal, if controversial, means to try to keep Mrs. Clinton's supporters from being motivated to vote.

The Trump team recently began a six-figure national ad campaign on urban radio stations, highlighting Mrs. Clinton's use of the word "superpredators."

"Why would Hillary Clinton call our children superpredators?" the ad's narrator asks, adding that Mrs. Clinton is "attacking our community."

"Hillary Clinton should be ashamed, using racially charged words describing black children as superpredators," the narrator says, adding that Mr. Trump will rebuild the community "using our labor, our spirit, our soul."

Campaign aides for Mr. Trump have talked in recent weeks about their efforts to discourage turnout for Mrs. Clinton.

While his aides insist publicly that victory is in sight, the approach represents a tacit admission that Mr. Trump, who has run a highly divisive and negative campaign and is viewed unfavorably by large percentages of minority and female voters, cannot expand his own vote total in a meaningful way.

The campaign's goal is to make Mrs. Clinton's vulnerabilities appear so disqualifying that her supporters should never consider voting for her.

Mr. Trump's attacks over the past several weeks have included suggesting that Mrs. Clinton uses drugs and linking her husband, former President Bill Clinton, to a decades-old rape allegation. A television commercial showed her coughing and stumbling and questioned whether she had the physical stamina to be president.

Much of the strategy, as described by a senior Trump aide who requested anonymity to divulge the campaign's internal plans, involves linking Mrs. Clinton to her husband's history of infidelity. More broadly, the campaign hopes it can taint her by reminding people of scandals in the couple's past. And when it can, it has tried to tie Mrs. Clinton to the shaming of some of the women who say they had affairs with Mr. Clinton.

The approach, the strategists believe, could be useful among millennial voters who used to support Senator Bernie Sanders of Vermont and are now unsure about Mrs. Clinton.

But Democrats and some Republicans do not believe the efforts will erode Mrs. Clinton's leads.

Trump Picks Voter ID Advocate for Election Fraud Panel

BY JULIE HIRSCHFELD DAVIS | MAY 11, 2017

WASHINGTON — President Trump on Thursday named Kris W. Kobach, the Kansas secretary of state who has pressed for aggressive measures to crack down on undocumented immigrants, to a commission investigating vote fraud, following through on his unsubstantiated claim that millions of "illegals" voted for his Democratic rival and robbed him of victory in the national popular vote.

Mr. Kobach, who has championed the strictest voter identification laws in the country, will be the vice chairman of the commission, which will be led by Vice President Mike Pence and is expected to include about a dozen others, including state officials from both political parties, said Sarah Huckabee Sanders, the deputy White House press secretary.

Mr. Trump signed an executive order on Thursday creating the commission, which Ms. Sanders said would have a broad mandate to review policies and practices that affect Americans' confidence in the integrity of federal elections. Marc E. Lotter, Mr. Pence's spokesman, said that voter suppression would be among the topics studied by the commission, which he said would take a wide-ranging look at problems at the state and national levels. But the order makes no mention of suppression or voting restrictions, specifying only "improper" or "fraudulent" registration and voting as issues to be explored.

Democrats and civil rights groups condemned the panel as a taxpayer-funded witch hunt, and the American Civil Liberties Union filed a legal request to the White House for records showing "concrete evidence" of fraudulent voting that would warrant the creation of such a commission.

"President Trump is attempting to spread his own fake news about election integrity," said Dale Ho, the director of the A.C.L.U.'s Voting

Rights Project. "If the Trump administration really cares about election integrity, it will divulge its supposed evidence before embarking on this commission boondoggle."

The commission was created at a tumultuous time in the White House, after Mr. Trump's abrupt firing on Tuesday of James B. Comey, the F.B.I. director, who had been leading an investigation into possible ties between the Trump campaign and Russia. United States intelligence agencies have concluded that Russia worked to sway the election to Mr. Trump.

Ms. Sanders said the group would produce a report for Mr. Trump next year on "system vulnerabilities that lead to improper registrations and voting." Its roots lie in Mr. Trump's own long-festering grievances and his conviction that illegal voting — including ballots cast by people who were registered to vote in multiple states, were not citizens, or were impersonating people whose names had remained on voting rolls after they died — reduced his margin of victory.

There is no evidence to support Mr. Trump's claims, which have been discredited repeatedly by fact-checkers, that millions of people voted illegally in 2016.

As a candidate, Mr. Trump repeatedly raised doubts about the integrity of the American voting system. After winning the election, he told members of Congress privately that three million to five million undocumented immigrants had voted illegally for Hillary Clinton, costing him the popular vote. And he promised to begin a major investigation.

Voting officials in both parties and academics across the country have long rejected the notion that fraudulent voting is widespread, finding instead that it is a sporadic and uncommon occurrence that has had no discernible effect on election outcomes. Mr. Trump's own lawyers concluded as much about the 2016 contest, asserting in legal filings that it was "not tainted" as they sought to block recounts in Michigan, Pennsylvania and Wisconsin.

"There are problems in the registration system that don't translate into fraud, there are sporadic and very rare instances of fraud, and voter impersonation fraud is the rarest of all," said Nathaniel Persily, a professor of political science at Stanford who served as the research director of the bipartisan Presidential Commission on Election Administration in 2012.

"The notion that there is widespread voting by undocumented immigrants or other ineligible voters has been studied repeatedly and found to be false," he said.

Mr. Kobach's influential position on the panel intensified the controversy over its creation, particularly among immigration advocacy and civil rights groups, as well as Democrats who said they feared he would use the perch to try to prevent minority voters from casting ballots.

"Selecting Kris Kobach as vice chair reveals exactly the kind of discriminatory witch hunt the American people can expect from this commission," said Representative Nancy Pelosi, Democrat of California and the House minority leader. "The president's 'election integrity' commission is clearly intended to accelerate the vile voter suppression efforts in states across the nation."

Mr. Kobach was the driving force behind a Kansas law requiring new voters to produce a passport, a birth certificate or naturalization papers as proof of citizenship. He worked last year to disqualify the state and local votes of thousands of people who did not meet those criteria. He has advocated the proof-of-citizenship requirement at the federal level as well, alleging rampant voter fraud without producing proof of a widespread problem.

Mr. Kobach dismissed the criticism of him as a "silly reaction" and said he had no preconceived ideas of what the commission would find. He argued that there had been no previous national effort to gather "hard data," rather than survey-based research, to quantify voting problems.

"If there's no such thing as voter fraud, or voter fraud is insignificant, then the commission will be able to confirm that," Mr. Kobach said in an interview. "What are they afraid of? Why do they not want to know these numbers?"

Ms. Sanders said the commission would also include the Republicans Connie Lawson, the secretary of state of Indiana, and Kenneth Blackwell, who formerly held that post in Ohio, as well as two top Democratic election officials: William M. Gardner of New Hampshire and Matthew Dunlap of Maine. Christy McCormick, a Republican member of the nonpartisan U.S. Election Assistance Commission appointed by President Barack Obama, has also been selected to serve on the panel.

"The president's committed to the thorough review of registration and voting issues in federal elections, and that's exactly what this commission is tasked with doing," Ms. Sanders said. "The commission will review policies and practices that enhance or undermine the American people's confidence in the integrity of federal elections and provide the president with a report that identifies system vulnerabilities that lead to improper registrations and voting."

Civil rights groups reacted with alarm to the creation of the task force, arguing that Mr. Trump's own claims of illegal voting by immigrants suggested that his intent was to work to restrict the voting rights of minorities.

Sherrilyn Ifill, the president of the NAACP Legal Defense and Educational Fund, called the commission "a thinly veiled voter suppression task force," adding that it was "designed to impugn the integrity of African-American and Latino participation in the political process."

Democratic lawmakers said the commission was ill-conceived at best and a potential front for discriminatory policies at worst.

"Instead of focusing on the myth of voter fraud, the president should be looking at ways to make it easier for eligible Americans to vote, given how difficult it is for some individuals to vote in this country," said Senator Benjamin A. Cardin, Democrat of Maryland.

Senator Chuck Schumer of New York, the minority leader, said the president was "chasing a unicorn" with taxpayer money and "perpetuating the dangerous myth that widespread voter fraud exists."

Asked for Voters' Data, States Give Trump Panel a Bipartisan 'No'

BY MICHAEL WINES | JUNE 30, 2017

A WHITE HOUSE COMMISSION'S sweeping request for the personal and public data of the nation's 200 million voters set off an avalanche of opposition by state leaders in both parties on Friday, as officials from California to Mississippi called the move an overreach and more than 20 states declared they would not comply.

It was an inauspicious start for the panel, which was created after President Trump claimed last winter that millions of illegal votes had robbed him of a popular-vote victory over Hillary Clinton.

The vice chairman and day-to-day leader of the Presidential Advisory Commission on Voter Integrity, Kris Kobach, had asked election officials in a letter to turn over the data "if publicly available," apparently to aid a nationwide search for evidence of election irregularities. Besides election information like voters' names and party affiliations, the commission sought personal information including birth dates, felony conviction records, voting histories for the past decade and the last four digits of all voters' Social Security numbers.

Mr. Kobach, the secretary of state in Kansas, has said he wants to match voter information with other data, like federal records of foreign residents and undocumented immigrants, to spotlight people who cast illegal ballots. He asserts that such fraud is widespread in Kansas and elsewhere, although he has found scant evidence of it so far.

But a growing number of state election officials have indicated — sometimes politely, sometimes brusquely — that they will not or cannot comply. Among them, ironically, were Mr. Kobach himself and a second member of the commission, Secretary of State Connie Lawson of Indiana, both of whom disclosed on Friday that privacy laws prevented them from furnishing some personal voter data.

By Friday, an informal tally by voting-rights advocates indicated that election officials in at least 22 states had partly or completely rejected the commission's request.

California, Massachusetts, Virginia, New York and Kentucky all quickly rejected the request. Other states, like Connecticut and Tennessee, said state law barred them from turning over some data. Wisconsin pledged to provide what it legally could, if the commission paid the $12,500 fee charged to anyone who copies the voter rolls.

Kentucky's secretary of state, Alison Lundergan Grimes, said that Mr. Trump's premise for creating the commission in the first place — that voter fraud was pervasive and needed to be reined in — was itself a fraud.

"Kentucky will not aid a commission that is at best a waste of taxpayer money and at worst an effort to legitimize voter suppression efforts across the country," Ms. Grimes, a Democrat, wrote in response to Mr. Kobach's request.

The pushback was bipartisan: The Mississippi secretary of state, Delbert Hosemann, a Republican, said Friday that he had not received a request from the commission, but colorfully suggested he would not honor one if it came.

"My reply would be: They can go jump in the Gulf of Mexico, and Mississippi is a great state to launch from," Mr. Hosemann said in a statement. "Mississippi residents should celebrate Independence Day and our state's right to protect the privacy of our citizens by conducting our own electoral processes."

Mr. Kobach, whose spokeswoman did not respond to phone and email messages, told The Kansas City Star on Friday that he was not concerned by other states' refusals to disclose voters' personal data. "That's perfectly fine," the newspaper quoted him as saying. "We understand that. And that is entirely up to each state."

In an interview last week with The Washington Times, Mr. Kobach said the accusations from voting-rights advocates and Democrats that the commission is a pretense for a voter-suppression enterprise designed to benefit Republicans were "complete and utter nonsense." Mr. Kobach told the newspaper that the act of collecting data posed no threat to voters, saying that the commission intended to match voter rolls with the federal government's database of noncitizens — including permanent residents, undocumented immigrants who had been apprehended and others — in a search for fraudulent ballots.

Much of the voter data sought by the commission — which is formally led by Vice President Mike Pence, as its chairman — is either public information or is routinely provided to political parties, researchers and others. But at least in California, some of it is protected by law from disclosure, said Alex Padilla, the secretary of state. And the personal data sought by the commission has never been aggregated on a national level with voting information, and should not be, he said.

Beyond concerns about privacy and how the data would be used, said Mr. Padilla, a Democrat, "I don't want Kris Kobach to do to California what he's done to Kansas."

Mr. Kobach, a Republican, has claimed voter fraud is rampant in Kansas, particularly by unauthorized immigrants. He has pushed for an array of restrictions on voting and registration — some of them overturned after legal battles — that a federal judge said had kept thousands of Kansans off the rolls.

Academic research and reports by the states themselves have repeatedly concluded that voter fraud is exceedingly rare and limited largely to absentee ballots and vote-rigging by election officials. But some scholars and advocates suspect that the commission's true goal is to paint a portrait of a voting system vulnerable to manipulation, regardless of the actual prevalence of fraud.

"I think the endgame here is to provide the pretext for federal legislation to make it harder for people to register and vote," Richard L. Hasen, a professor and elections expert at the University of California, Irvine School of Law, said in an interview.

Mr. Hasen and some voting-rights advocates say they anticipate that the commission's findings will be followed by Republican legislation to amend the 1993 National Voter Registration Act — the so-called motor voter law, a longtime target of Republican complaints.

New legislation could give states more leeway to impose voting preconditions like proof of citizenship and to make it easier for officials to purge inactive voters from the rolls, Mr. Hasen said.

The commission is officially bipartisan, and Mr. Kobach has said he will bring no biases to the job. That said, the Republicans named to the panel so far include some of the most ardent advocates of voting restrictions, led by Mr. Kobach and J. Kenneth Blackwell, who pushed for more stringent voting rules in the mid-2000s as Ohio secretary of state.

Another Republican appointee announced on Thursday, Hans A. von Spakovsky, is a former Justice Department official in the George W. Bush administration who advocates stricter laws on voting and registering. Mr. von Spakovsky, a Heritage Foundation scholar who maintains an online repository of voting-fraud convictions, has crusaded against what he calls a liberal bias in federal enforcement of election laws. "When it comes to American elections, the Obama Justice Department has taken the side of criminals over law-abiding citizens," he wrote last year in a critique of the department's lawyers. "It has used selective enforcement of the law to help Democrats retain power."

Voting-rights advocates have urged Democrats to shun membership on the commission, but Maine's secretary of state, Matthew Dunlap, agreed to join it this month — in part, he said in an interview, to serve as a watchdog.

"If it takes a dishonest turn, say, and instead of having our thesis informed by facts we have our facts informed by the thesis, I'm in an incredible position to talk about that publicly," Mr. Dunlap said.

Trump Disbands Commission on Voter Fraud

BY MICHAEL TACKETT AND MICHAEL WINES | JAN. 3, 2018

WASHINGTON — President Trump on Wednesday abruptly shut down a White House commission he had charged with investigating voter fraud, ending a brief quest for evidence of election theft that generated lawsuits, outrage and some scholarly testimony, but no real evidence that American elections are corrupt.

On Thursday, Mr. Trump called for requiring voter identification in a pair of Twitter posts because the voting system "is rigged." "Push hard for Voter Identification!" Mr. Trump wrote.

Mr. Trump did not acknowledge the commission's inability to find evidence of fraud, but cast the closing as a result of continuing legal challenges.

"Despite substantial evidence of voter fraud, many states have refused to provide the Presidential Advisory Commission on Election Integrity with basic information relevant to its inquiry," Mr. Trump said in a White House statement on Wednesday.

"Rather than engage in endless legal battles at taxpayer expense, today I signed an executive order to dissolve the commission, and have asked the Department of Homeland Security to review these issues and determine next courses of action," he said.

In fact, no state has uncovered significant evidence to support the president's claim, and election officials, including many Republicans, have strongly rejected it.

Mr. Trump established the commission after his repeated insistence, without credible evidence, that widespread voter fraud explained how Hillary Clinton received about 2.9 million more votes while he won the presidency in the Electoral College.

It is an issue that continues to resonate with his base voters, and

Mr. Trump has mentioned it in recent rallies, but there have been few Republicans in Congress who have followed him.

The closing of the commission was a blow for Kris Kobach, the secretary of state of Kansas and the panel's vice chairman. Mr. Kobach was one of a few state officials to support Mr. Trump's contention of widespread fraud.

But Mr. Kobach insisted in an interview that the commission's work would not end but rather would be transferred to the Department of Homeland Security, one of the federal agencies charged with ensuring election integrity and one that he said critics would find more difficult to target.

As a White House commission, the voter-fraud panel was subject to public-disclosure requirements and other restrictions that Mr. Kobach said opponents of the inquiry had seized on in "a determined effort by the left" to hamstring its investigation. At last count, he said, the panel faced at least eight lawsuits accusing it of ignoring various federal requirements, including one from a commission member, Matthew Dunlap, the Maine secretary of state, that claimed he had been illegally excluded from its deliberations.

"It got to the point where the staff of the commission was spending more time responding to litigation than doing an investigation," Mr. Kobach said. "Think of it as an option play; a decision was made in the middle of the day to pass the ball. The Department of Homeland Security is going to be able to move faster and more efficiently than a presidential advisory commission."

A spokesman for homeland security, Tyler Q. Houlton, said on Wednesday that "the department continues to focus our efforts on securing elections against those who seek to undermine the election system or its integrity."

"We will do this in support of state governments who are responsible for administering elections," he added.

But states may well not cooperate with the department any more than they did with the panel.

As a first step, Mr. Kobach, who said he would remain as an informal adviser to homeland security, said the department would marshal its files on immigrants, legal and otherwise, so that they can be matched with lists of registered voters nationwide to detect foreign citizens who are illegally casting ballots in American elections. Both Mr. Trump and Mr. Kobach have insisted that voting by noncitizens is endemic — Mr. Trump falsely claimed that millions of illegal voters cost him a popular-vote victory in 2016 — but investigations, including ones by Mr. Kobach and the Justice Department under President George W. Bush, turned up scant evidence of fraud.

Many Democratic secretaries of state had said they believed the commission had a goal of laying the groundwork for restrictions that will mostly make it harder for traditional Democratic constituencies — minorities, young people and the poor — to cast ballots, which would benefit Republican candidates.

The commission had been seeking voluminous information on voters, including names, addresses, dates of birth, political affiliations and the last four digits of Social Security numbers, along with voting history. It also had requested records of felony convictions and whether voters are registered in other states.

But many states bar the release of even partial Social Security numbers or other personal information because that data can be used for identity theft.

The commission had faced a deadline days from now about how it would proceed. Vice President Mike Pence, who was tasked with running it, was never particularly excited about the idea, and several members of the commission had objected to working with Mr. Kobach, according to a White House official.

Another official said that the idea, which was supported by the president's former chief strategist, Stephen K. Bannon, was destined to be shoved off on an agency. And on a day when Mr. Bannon was already under fire for disparaging comments he made in a new book about the presidency, aides put the blame for the existence of the commission on him and insisted he had supported it eagerly. As coverage of the book dominated headlines, the White House pushed out the news of the commission's closing.

Groups that opposed the commission said its real mission was voter suppression, in ways that would help Republicans, and they were quick to declare victory.

"The commission's entire purpose was to legitimize voter suppression," said Vanita Gupta, the president of the Leadership Conference on Civil and Human Rights and former head of the Justice Department's Civil Rights Division.

"The abrupt abandonment of the commission makes clear that it had become a thoroughly discredited body that could not find evidence of mass voter fraud," Ms. Gupta said. "The commission itself was unable to justify its existence as a result."

In a telephone interview late Wednesday, Mr. Dunlap, a Democrat and a member of the panel who has consistently criticized the commission's operations, said the White House's decision to move the inquiry to the Department of Homeland Security was "utterly alarming."

"Homeland security operates very much in the dark," he said. "Any chance of having this investigation done in a public forum is now lost, and I think people should be, frankly, frightened by that."

While the conduct of elections now rests with state officials, he said, "Secretary Kobach wants homeland security to make those decisions without public input. That's the real threat from this decision."

The Senate Democratic leader, Chuck Schumer of New York, said in a statement that "the commission never had anything to do with election integrity. It was instead a front to suppress the vote, perpetrate dangerous and baseless claims, and was ridiculed from one end of the country to the other."

Richard L. Hasen, a law professor and election law scholar at the University of California, Irvine, was sharply critical of the commission in a blog post.

"The commission was poorly organized and conceived," he wrote.

He added, "It made rookie, boneheaded mistakes about handling documents used by the commission, again in violation of federal law. It did not seem to have an endgame."

MATTHEW HAAG and MAGGIE HABERMAN contributed reporting from New York, and RON NIXON from Washington.

Strict North Carolina Voter ID Law Thwarted After Supreme Court Rejects Case

BY ADAM LIPTAK AND MICHAEL WINES | MAY 15, 2017

WASHINGTON — The Supreme Court on Monday refused to revive a restrictive North Carolina voting law that a federal appeals court had struck down as an unconstitutional effort to "target African-Americans with almost surgical precision."

The court's decision not to hear an appeal in the case effectively overturned one of the most far-reaching attempts by Republicans to counter what they contended, without evidence, was widespread voter fraud in North Carolina. The law rejected the forms of identification used disproportionately by blacks, including IDs issued to government employees, students and people receiving public assistance.

Democrats and civil rights groups, wary of the Supreme Court now that it has regained a conservative majority with the appointment of Justice Neil M. Gorsuch, welcomed the announcement that it would not hear the case.

"An ugly chapter in voter suppression is finally closing," said Dale Ho, director of the A.C.L.U.'s Voting Rights Project.

The leaders of North Carolina's Republican-controlled Legislature vowed that they would seek to enact new voting restrictions after their defeat.

"All North Carolinians can rest assured that Republican legislators will continue fighting to protect the integrity of our elections by implementing the common sense requirement to show a photo ID when we vote," House Speaker Tim Moore and Phil Berger, the president pro tempore of the North Carolina Senate, said in a statement.

But their options will be limited by the appeals court decision and will most likely face opposition from Gov. Roy Cooper, a Democrat who welcomed the Supreme Court's decision not to hear the appeal.

"Today's announcement is good news for North Carolina voters," Mr. Cooper said in a statement. "We need to be making it easier to vote, not harder."

The divisions in the state's leadership, which led to a dispute about who represented the state in the case, figured in the Supreme Court's decision not to hear it, Chief Justice John G. Roberts Jr. wrote in a statement that accompanied the court's one-sentence order. He added that nothing should be read into the court's decision to decline to hear the case.

The Supreme Court's action set no precedent and will have no impact in most of the country. But it let stand the United States Court of Appeals for the Fourth Circuit's sweeping rejection of an array of voting restrictions by North Carolina.

The law, enacted by the state legislature in 2013, imposed a range of voting restrictions, including the new voter identification requirements. It was part of a wave of voting restrictions enacted after a 5-to-4 Supreme Court decision that effectively struck down a central part of the federal Voting Rights Act, weakening federal oversight of voting rights.

The case challenging the North Carolina law was brought by civil rights groups and the Obama administration. A trial judge rejected arguments that the law violated the Constitution and what remained of the Voting Rights Act. But a three-judge panel of the appeals court disagreed.

The appeals court ruling struck down five parts of the law: its voter ID requirements, a rollback of early voting to 10 days from 17, an elimination of same-day registration and of preregistration of some teenagers, and its ban on counting votes cast in the wrong precinct.

The court found that all five restrictions "disproportionately affected African-Americans." The law's voter identification provision, for instance, "retained only those types of photo ID disproportionately held by whites and excluded those disproportionately held by African-Americans."

That was the case, the court said, even though the state had "failed to identify even a single individual who has ever been charged with committing in-person voter fraud in North Carolina." But it did find that there was evidence of fraud in absentee voting by mail, a method used disproportionately by white voters. The Legislature, however, exempted absentee voting from the photo ID requirement.

The court also found that the early voting restrictions had a much larger effect on black voters, who "disproportionately used the first seven days of early voting." The law, the court said, eliminated one of two "souls to the polls" Sundays, when black churches provided rides to polling places.

Voting rights advocates had been watching the North Carolina case for signs of how a closely divided Supreme Court would rule on similar lawsuits now that Justice Gorsuch is on the court.

In September, a deadlocked Supreme Court turned down an emergency pre-election request from state officials to block the appeals court's ruling. Justices Ruth Bader Ginsburg, Stephen G. Breyer, Sonia Sotomayor and Elena Kagan voted to reject the state's arguments. Chief Justice Roberts and Justices Anthony M. Kennedy, Clarence Thomas and Samuel A. Alito Jr. would have temporarily reinstated parts of the law.

The decision on Monday not to hear the case turned on procedural issues, not on the substance of the suit, so the court's current leanings remain unknown.

State officials asked the Supreme Court in December to hear their appeal in the case, North Carolina v. North Carolina State Conference of the NAACP, No. 16-833.

Two months later, in an unusual last-minute procedural maneuver, two newly elected Democratic officials — Mr. Cooper and Attorney General Josh Stein — asked the court to dismiss the state's petition seeking review. Lawyers for the General Assembly opposed the motion.

In his statement on Monday, Chief Justice Roberts said the Supreme Court's decision to decline to grant the petition seeking review, or petition for certiorari, turned on that dispute.

"Given the blizzard of filings over who is and who is not authorized to seek review in this Court under North Carolina law," the chief justice wrote, quoting an earlier decision, "it is important to recall our frequent admonition that 'the denial of a writ of certiorari imports no expression of opinion upon the merits of the case.' "

Civil liberties advocates, nevertheless, called it a victory for voting rights and — for now, at least — a precedent with broad application.

"This is the law of the land in the Fourth Circuit," said Daniel T. Donovan, a lawyer for the plaintiffs.

The justices are likely to take a more definitive position on voting rights issues when and if they hear one of several cases that appear bound for the court. The most likely candidate is a lawsuit challenging Texas' 2011 voter identification law.

A federal district judge ruled in April that the Texas Legislature had intentionally discriminated against black and Hispanic voters when it enacted the law.

ADAM LIPTAK reported from Washington, and **MICHAEL WINES** from New York.

Texas' Voter ID Law Does Not Discriminate and Can Stand, Appeals Panel Rules

BY MANNY FERNANDEZ | APRIL 27, 2018

HOUSTON — A federal appeals court upheld Texas' voter identification law on Friday, saying that it does not discriminate against black and Hispanic voters.

The decision by a three-judge panel of the United States Court of Appeals for the Fifth Circuit, in New Orleans, overturned a lower-court ruling that had struck down the law. It was the latest milestone in a yearslong legal battle over the state's efforts to require voters to show government-issued identification in order to cast a ballot.

The panel's decision, by a vote of 2 to 1, was the first time a federal court had upheld the law, a revamped version of one of the toughest voter ID restrictions in the country.

The original law, which was known as Senate Bill 14 and was passed by the Republican-dominated Texas Legislature in 2011, required voters to show a driver's license, passport or other government-issued photo ID before casting a ballot. The law took effect in 2013, and it was found by the same federal appellate court to have a discriminatory effect on black and Hispanic voters, many of whom lack government-issued photo ID.

The Legislature then loosened the restrictions last year by passing a new law, known as Senate Bill 5, that allowed voters who lacked one of the seven approved forms of ID to cast a ballot if they signed an affidavit stating why they could not obtain an approved ID. Those voters must show an alternative form of identification, including a utility bill or a bank statement.

Last year, a federal district court judge struck down the new law. But the Fifth Circuit later allowed the law to go into effect in January while it considered the state's appeal.

One of the most contentious issues with the new law is that it creates criminal penalties for those who make false statements in their sworn affidavits, a move that critics of the law believe confuses and frightens potential voters.

In the ruling on Friday, the three-judge panel said concerns that the criminal penalties would intimidate voters were "wholly speculative." The judges wrote that the Legislature had "succeeded in its goal" of passing a new law "designed to cure all the flaws" of the original.

The case had previously raised the possibility that the state's election procedures could be put back under federal oversight, in a process called preclearance. It was a potential legal penalty for Texas after a lower court judge had found that the state had intentionally discriminated against minority voters. But on Friday, the Fifth Circuit panel appeared to take preclearance off the table, ruling that "there is no equitable basis for subjecting Texas to ongoing federal election scrutiny."

Republican leaders in Texas, who have denied that the law discriminates and have defended it as a means of preventing voter fraud, applauded the decision.

"The court rightly recognized that when the Legislature passed Senate Bill 5 last session, it complied with every change the Fifth Circuit ordered to the original voter ID law," the Texas attorney general, Ken Paxton, said in a statement. "Safeguarding the integrity of our elections is essential to preserving our democracy. The revised voter ID law removes any burden on voters who cannot obtain a photo ID."

An appeal by the plaintiffs — a group of Democratic lawmakers, individual voters and black, Hispanic and civil-rights organizations that sued Texas — seemed likely. They can appeal to either the full Fifth Circuit or to the Supreme Court.

"Our view today is the same as it has been since the first day of this litigation — Texas' voter ID law is discriminatory," said State Representative Rafael Anchia, a Dallas Democrat who is the chairman of the Mexican American Legislative Caucus, one of the plaintiffs in the lawsuit. "We are undeterred by today's decision, and we will continue to fight against laws that aim to suppress the vote."

Kristen Clarke, the president and executive director of the Lawyers' Committee for Civil Rights Under Law, which is part of the legal team representing the plaintiffs, said an appeal was "one option on the table."

"No law should be allowed to stand that is merely built on the back of a plainly discriminatory law," Ms. Clarke said.

Richard L. Hasen, an election law expert and law professor at the University of California, Irvine, said the decision seemed to preclude Texas from preclearance. But he added that the possibility of federal oversight of Texas election procedures still existed in another case, the state's redistricting legal battle, which is now before the Supreme Court.

"But no doubt this is a big blow for those who think Texas needs federal supervision," Professor Hasen said.

The Myths of Voter ID

OPINION | BY ROSS DOUTHAT | FEB. 12, 2019

A new study confirms that the polarized debate over voter identification isn't that important.

USUALLY WHEN SOME sententious centrist talks about ending partisan polarization and just coming up with "solutions" based on "data" or "studies" or "expert consensus," the appropriate response is to roll your eyes — the way people have been eye-rolling lately at Howard Schultz of Starbucks and his apparently substance-free vision for an independent presidential campaign. Usually where you find polarization, you also find some issue of great moment, some important conflict of interests or values, that can't just be turned over to the smart people to solve because any "solution" would inevitably be a victory for one side and a defeat for the other.

But there are occasional exceptions: Polarizing issues where you could essentially call a truce without anyone winning or losing, without it affecting the balance of power in America's political debates and culture wars, without anything disappearing except a lot of nonsense, hysteria and panic.

My candidate for the exception is the debate over voter ID laws. For as long as I've been politically conscious, conservatives have touted tougher identification requirements at the polls as a means to fight the scourge of voter fraud, and over the last decade Republicans have successfully implemented voter ID laws in a number of reddish states. Over the same period those laws have been cited by liberals as evidence that Republicans are bent on winning elections by disenfranchising Democrats — locking out poor and minority voters in a rerun of the Jim Crow-poll tax era, and electing conservative politicians at the expense of democracy itself.

You could imagine a world in which the voter ID debate reflected a real and sweeping clash of interests. If conservatives were right that the laws reduced rampant voter fraud by preventing illegal immigrants from voting for Democrats in large numbers, and meanwhile liberals were also right that the laws dramatically reduced turnout among African-Americans and other liberal-leaning constituencies, effectively limiting the right to vote, then the whole debate would be extremely consequential and difficult to resolve.

In this world, however, the stakes seem to be considerably lower. That's the conclusion of a new study, one of the largest to date, from the economists Enrico Cantoni and Vincent Pons, which assessed the impact of voter ID laws between 2008 and 2016 using a nationwide voter file. The study finds that requiring voter identification has no effect on turnout — not overall, and not on "any group defined by race, gender, age, or party affiliation."

If that shocks you, it shouldn't. The evidence that voter ID laws meaningfully suppress minority votes has always been shaky; a literature review in 2017 that filtered out studies with obvious design flaws reported "modest, if any, turnout effects of voter identification laws" in the best research on the subject. So a voter ID requirement might possibly affect the closest of close races, based on what we've learned up till now — but if the Cantoni and Pons results hold up, the real effect is basically nil.

But before conservatives claim vindication, the new paper also casts doubt on the argument for voter ID laws, finding no effect on fraud itself, nor even any effect on public confidence in the integrity of the ballot. Which should be even less surprising than the absence of evidence for voter suppression, because since the George W. Bush administration a large group of people with strong incentives to uncover voter fraud — Republican lawmakers, law-enforcement personnel and conservative election researchers — have failed to produce any evidence that the problem exists on a scale that requires a legislative response. And the rare prosecuted cases generally seem disproportionate to the offense involved — with confused individuals in the dock rather than old-fashioned Chicago-style machines.

There is more to the voting-rights debate than just voter ID laws; nothing in the new study settles arguments about early voting, absentee balloting and more. Still, because the ID debate is a particular flash point, its findings are a real public service. No matter where you stand on the voter fraud-voter suppression controversies, these findings strengthen the case for dialing down outrage, reducing anxiety and generally recognizing that if we stopped pushing for these laws *and* stopped freaking out about how they supposedly doom democracy, voting in America would rattle along basically unchanged.

But since it's conservatives and Republicans who are the prime mover here, because they're generally the ones pushing legal changes, they also have the primary obligation to step back and stand down.

Despite what many liberals believe, much of the right's anxiety about voter fraud is sincere, not just a cynical cover for racist vote suppression. I have had enough arguments with fellow conservatives on this issue to attest that the specter of those old Chicago operations haunts the right, along with more contemporary fears generated by a left that really does want to extend some of the benefits of citizenship to illegal immigrants.

At the same time there's also no question that a lot of Republican operatives pushing voter ID laws are cynics who expect their party to benefit from lower minority turnout, and a number of professional right-wing partisans — including our president — see an upside in frightening their voters or viewers with the racialized threat of "urban" ballot-stuffing.

Which, again, is what makes the evidence from this study so helpful: It offers reasons for both the conservative sincerely worried about voter fraud and the operative cynically hoping for lower Democratic turnout to let this issue slide.

And in letting it slide, Republicans might even have more to gain than Democrats. After all, the cynical side of the voter ID push is pretty transparent, meaning that even if the laws don't have real vote-suppressing consequences, they do serve as a continuing gesture of disrespect to minority voters, a continuing expression of G.O.P. indifference to the African-American memory of what vote restrictions used to mean. So their removal from the Republican agenda could be an act of minority outreach unto itself.

Maybe that's too optimistic. But even without that upside, the case for standing down is strong. The voter ID debate essentially involves Republicans whipping themselves into a panic over a problem that doesn't meaningfully affect their chances of winning elections, and then passing laws that whip Democrats into a panic over a problem that also doesn't meaningfully affect their chances of winning elections. So if the debate simply disappeared tomorrow, a source of distrust would vanish without either side losing ground. There are few cases where that's possible. Let's seize this one.

ROSS DOUTHAT has been an Opinion columnist for The Times since 2009. He is the author of several books, most recently, "To Change the Church: Pope Francis and the Future of Catholicism."

CHAPTER 3

Other Voter Suppression Tactics

Voter suppression can take many forms beyond ID requirements. Many states purge their voter rolls of inactive voters, who are often the exact people that campaigns want to inspire to vote again. People may be discouraged from voting if it's burdensome — for example, if there aren't enough polling places or long enough voting hours. Others may feel their vote doesn't matter or won't be counted. All of these processes can intimidate voters, inspire distrust in the democratic process and drive down voter turnout.

Voters Fear Their Ballot Won't Count, Poll Shows

BY GIOVANNI RUSSONELLO | OCT. 25, 2016

FEWER THAN HALF of Americans are very confident that their vote for president will be counted correctly — and most say their ballot will not matter anyway because the political process is so dominated by corporate interests.

These are among the results of a P.R.R.I. poll released on Tuesday showing a nation that is deeply ambivalent about the electoral process.

Americans are almost evenly divided on whether fraud or voter repression is a bigger problem, despite many studies showing that fraud is almost nonexistent nationwide.

The findings suggest there may be at least some audience for Donald J. Trump's claims that the presidential election could be "rigged."

And they dovetail with recent trends. In a Gallup survey in August, 36 percent of Americans said that voter fraud would most likely be a major problem this election, more than those who said it would not be an issue. That was up significantly from a pre-election Gallup poll in 2004, when just 24 percent expressed serious concern about fraud.

"Most pernicious, I think, is the fact that Americans are basically divided on which is the bigger problem, voter fraud or disenfranchisement," said Robert P. Jones, the chief executive of P.R.R.I.

In the poll, 41 percent said voter suppression was a bigger issue, while 37 percent named fraud.

"All the studies we have point to voter fraud being essentially a negligible problem," Mr. Jones said. "Yet people are just as worried about that as they are about something we have a long history of, which is eligible voters being denied the right to vote. That's certainly a perception problem."

Just 43 percent of Americans in the survey expressed a great deal of confidence that their vote would be counted correctly. By nearly 30 points, supporters of Hillary Clinton were more likely to feel confident than Trump backers.

But political independents were the most skeptical, with just over a third expressing a great deal of confidence.

Independents were also among the most likely to say that the influence of wealthy interests overpowered voting.

Fully 57 percent of all Americans, and nearly two-thirds of independents, agreed that "politics and elections are controlled by people with money and by big corporations," so it does not matter if they vote.

At 66 percent, young people are among the most likely to feel pessimistic about the worth of their vote. "This goes along with a lot of what we know about millennials, that they distrust institutions in general," Mr. Jones said. "But it doesn't bode well for civic participation going forward."

Mr. Trump's repeated insistence that the election could be rigged brings to a head more than a decade of work by conservative groups to combat what they say is a widespread problem: ballots being cast by ineligible or repeat voters. The Supreme Court in 2013 annulled a major provision of the Voting Rights Act, and this election, 14 states have new laws in place that restrict who can cast a ballot, according to the Brennan Center for Justice.

"In many different ways, voters rightly perceive that the system isn't working that well — whether it's gerrymandered districts leaving little competition, or a campaign finance system giving big money even greater power," said Michael Waldman, president of the Brennan Center and author of "The Fight to Vote."

"They see these voting issues sometimes along the same lines," Mr. Waldman added. "The public is not wrong that there's a general, vital need to upgrade our democracy. It just is the case that voter fraud isn't actually one of the problems."

The survey depicts a nation broadly dispirited with the political process. About three-quarters of Americans say the country is going in the wrong direction.

And for both Mrs. Clinton and Mr. Trump, a majority of their supporters say they are casting ballots mostly in opposition to the other candidate, not in favor of their own. Asked which candidate better understands the problems of people like them, voters were most likely to say neither, with about four in 10 selecting this option.

The poll was conducted Sept. 1 to 27, online and via telephone, among 2,010 respondents to NORC's AmeriSpeak Panel, which uses a probability sample. The margin of sampling error is plus or minus three percentage points.

Five Ways Republicans Are Threatening Voting Rights

OPINION | BY ANNA NORTH | NOV. 7, 2016

DONALD TRUMP HAS been claiming for months now that Tuesday's election will be "rigged." But the only ones threatening the democratic process are Mr. Trump, with his thinly veiled calls for voter suppression, and Republicans in state governments doing their utmost to keep minority voters from the polls. Below are five ways the candidate and the Republican Party are working to suppress voting this year, drawn from recent editorials:

VOTER ID LAWS

Republicans have repeatedly raised concerns about voter fraud — which is essentially nonexistent in the United States — as justification for voter ID laws that disproportionately affect poor people, minorities and students.

This year will be the first presidential election since the Supreme Court struck down a major part of the Voting Rights Act in 2013, meaning many areas with a history of racial discrimination in voting would no longer have to clear new voting laws with the federal government. After that decision, several states enacted new restrictions, including voter ID laws.

There's some good news, though: A North Dakota judge in August ordered the state to stop enforcing its voter ID law, which could have disenfranchised nearly 4,000 Native American residents. Courts in Wisconsin, Kansas and Ohio have also dealt blows to voter ID laws.

EARLY VOTING RESTRICTIONS

In North Carolina, where a court in July struck down a 2013 voter ID law whose restrictions took aim at black voters, Republicans on local election boards are busily cutting back early and Sunday voting hours, which are disproportionately used by African-Americans.

LIMITING AUTOMATIC REGISTRATION

Gov. Bruce Rauner of Illinois in August vetoed a bill that would have allowed automatic voter registration at motor vehicle offices and added as many as two million new voters to the rolls starting in 2018.

DISENFRANCHISING PEOPLE WITH CONVICTIONS

Almost six million Americans will be denied the right to vote on Tuesday because of criminal convictions. Many of them are victims of laws enacted in Southern states specifically to disenfranchise African-Americans. Three-quarters of Americans believe people who have served their time should have their voting rights restored, but Republicans in Virginia and elsewhere are fighting to keep people with convictions from voting.

CONDONING VOTER INTIMIDATION

As Republicans at the state level ramp up voter suppression efforts, Mr. Trump has been telling his supporters to watch "certain areas" on Election Days, essentially inviting them to intimidate minority voters. While the Republican National Committee has said it doesn't condone voter intimidation, it has also made it "very clear that the R.N.C. is in full coordination with the Trump campaign."

Voters who run into problems or have questions on Election Day can call 866-OUR-VOTE, a nonpartisan hotline, for help.

ANNA NORTH is a member of the editorial board.

Spread of Early Voting Is Forging New Habits and Campaign Tactics

BY JEREMY W. PETERS | NOV. 7, 2016

IN 1977, A FLOOD control measure on the ballot in Monterey, Calif., became what historians say was the first modern American election decided by people who voted before Election Day.

It was a strange moment even for some who participated; elections had traditionally been a kind of civic gathering, on one day.

But the practice caught on with voters, and it eventually spread from the West Coast to 37 states and the District of Columbia. Today, at least 43 million Americans have already voted in the presidential election. And when the ballots are tallied nationwide Tuesday evening, more than one-third of them will have come from people who voted early — a record.

Voting before Election Day has become so commonplace that it is reshaping how campaigns are waged, and how Americans see the race in its final, frantic days.

"The idea that one wakes up and it's Election Day in America is actually a rather quaint idea now," said Russ Schriefer, a Republican consultant who has worked on presidential campaigns for two decades. "It is as much as a monthlong process to draw people in. And so your advertising tactics, your messaging tactics and certainly your ground game have changed completely."

The spread of early balloting is forging new habits that are forcing campaigns to rethink how they allocate their resources. And it tends to favor those campaigns that are more technologically sophisticated and can identify, draw out and measure its support over a longer voting period.

In Florida, a battleground state where just a few hundred votes can tip an election and victory can guarantee the White House, new behaviors are rapidly taking hold. Hispanics, who have tended to turn out mostly on Election Day, are voting earlier in much larger numbers this year, after a major Democratic-led effort to mobilize them. This is especially true among young and first-time Hispanic voters, who are just forming their voting habits and are likely to retain the practice of casting ballots early, according to those who study early voting.

That will mean that future campaigns will need to further adapt and dedicate more time and money to chasing votes up to six weeks before Election Day.

Until relatively recently, early voting was confined mostly to Western states. In 1978, California became the first state to allow anyone to cast an absentee ballot regardless of whether they were actually going to be absent on Election Day or not. Oregon held its first statewide vote-by-mail election in 1993. Washington State started allowing all its voters to apply for permanent absentee status around the same time.

The idea of a rolling election actually dates back to frontier times, when it would sometimes take days for people to reach their polling places. Then in 1845, Congress established one national Election Day. The reason, said Michael McDonald, an associate professor of political science at the University of Florida, should sound familiar: suspicion of fraud.

"People were concerned that you could vote in more than one location — basically the same reasons that are made against convenience voting today," he said.

Early voting has been expanding despite the political tensions that tend to infuse any debate over voting. Republicans often resist making voting more accessible — whether by opening more polling locations in the weeks before an election or allowing voters to mail in ballots — saying that the process could invite fraud. Republican-led legislatures in Ohio and North Carolina were successful in reducing early voting compared with 2012. Democrats, who generally favor fewer barriers and greater access, have sued to block those restrictions.

For campaigns today, the availability of real-time data on who has voted and when allows a nimble operation to determine whether those likely to support the candidate have turned out and redirect resources accordingly. Hillary Clinton's campaign has been particularly deft, scheduling concerts with Jennifer Lopez in Miami and Beyoncé in Cleveland, where Democrats have been focusing intensely on early turnout. The artists used the occasion not just to perform but to plead with fans to vote for Mrs. Clinton.

For the voter, that early turnout data is now ubiquitously covered in the news media, adding a new dynamic to the campaign horse race punditry. Of course, the data is not exact: It can show how many registered Republicans, Democrats and unaffiliated voters have cast ballots from a particular area, allowing political analysts to deduce which candidate is probably ahead.

Campaigns have long had access to similar data. But with much of the information now available on secretary of state websites all over the country, the tally of who is up and who is down in the early vote is breathlessly followed.

"This information has gone from the war room into the newsroom," said Paul Gronke, director of the early voter information center at Reed College. "We've gotten over the tipping point here in terms of the amount of coverage and attention dedicated to these numbers."

The availability of the information has led some prognosticators to declare races won or lost. Over the weekend in Nevada, one of the state's top political commentators said it would be all but impossible for Donald J. Trump to beat Mrs. Clinton there given how many more registered Democrats had already cast ballots than Republicans.

The rush to call a race before it is over raises difficult questions about whether having so much public information on early voting could interfere with elections.

"We don't know what that could do to depress turnout," Mr. Schriefer said.

So far, however, turnout has been robust. The reasons extend beyond the effectiveness of the methods that the campaigns are using to drive people to the polls.

One factor appears to be the concern that many voters have of being stuck for hours if they wait until the last minute on Election Day. "They have been told — rightly — that they can expect some long lines," said Allegra Chapman, director of voting and elections for Common Cause, which advocates more access to voting. "And they are being urged to take advantage of early voting as much as possible."

And there are other, less practical factors. Many voters just seem to want this election — one of the most divisive, bitter and strangest spectacles in recent political history — to be over.

"I thought that perhaps the ambivalence about the two major candidates might lead people to hold their ballots this year," Mr. Gronke said. "But the opposite seems to be happening. Voters are sick and tired of this election, the negative campaigning and the mudslinging, and are casting their ballots as soon as they can."

GIOVANNI RUSSONELLO contributed reporting.

Justices Won't Revive Order Barring Voter Intimidation in Ohio

BY ADAM LIPTAK | NOV. 7, 2016

WASHINGTON — The Supreme Court on Monday refused to intercede in a lawsuit brought by the Ohio Democratic Party against Donald J. Trump's presidential campaign. The justices turned away a last-minute bid from the party to reinstate a sweeping order from a trial judge that had barred the Trump campaign from harassing or intimidating voters in Ohio.

The Supreme Court's brief order gave no reasons for staying out of the case and did not note any dissents.

Justice Ruth Bader Ginsburg, who has been critical of Mr. Trump, added a brief statement explaining her vote in the case, Ohio Democratic Party v. Donald J. Trump for President.

She said that an Ohio law already forbids the harassment of voters, suggesting that a court order to enforce that law was not needed.

Mr. Trump has urged his supporters to act as poll observers, suggesting that voters in unspecified "certain areas" were likely to engage in fraud.

The Ohio Democratic Party sued the campaign, saying it sought "to vindicate the constitutional rights of voters to exercise the franchise free from intimidation."

At a hearing on Friday, Judge James S. Gwin of the Federal District Court in Cleveland said that there was no evidence to support Mr. Trump's assertions concerning voter fraud and that Mr. Trump had used "code words" to urge his supporters to intimidate voters likely to cast their ballots for Hillary Clinton.

"It's really an incitement to harass Democratic-leaning but more specifically African-American or Hispanic voters," Judge Gwin said at the hearing.

That same day, Judge Gwin issued a broad order barring people associated with the Trump campaign from harassing, challenging or taking pictures of voters.

The Trump campaign appealed, saying that the order was too broad and that it "tramples upon core First Amendment freedoms."

"One example illustrates the point," the campaign's brief said. "The order prohibits anyone from having a truthful discussion about voting rules with another voter when the two are heading inside to vote. Such a prohibition clearly violates the First Amendment."

On Sunday, a three-judge panel of the United States Court of Appeals for the Sixth Circuit, in Cincinnati, stayed Judge Gwin's order. The appeals court said Judge Gwin had abused his discretion in issuing it.

Late on Sunday, the Ohio Democratic Party asked the Supreme Court to intervene. It said that the Sixth Circuit had acted without full briefing and that Judge Gwin had acted with care.

Judge Gwin's order, the party's brief said, was "tailored precisely to match the evidence in the record of the plans by the campaign and its supporters to disrupt the voting process and intimidate voters."

How to Report Voter Intimidation, and How to Spot It

BY NIRAJ CHOKSHI | NOV. 6, 2018

WELL BEFORE ELECTION DAY, voters in Texas and North Carolina had already started reporting facing harassment.

The federal government prohibits such acts of intimidation, but what that entails isn't always clear. In some cases, it can mean threats of violence. In others, it can be attempts at coercion. This kind of harassment may be uncommon, but voting rights advocates say voters should be vigilant.

"I would say to people, 'Use your gut,' " said Virginia Kase, the chief executive of the nonpartisan League of Women Voters, which encourages democratic participation. "If it doesn't feel right, it probably isn't."

Here's a brief guide to voter intimidation and what to do about it.

WHAT IS VOTER INTIMIDATION?

Anyone who tries to "intimidate, threaten, or coerce" individuals to interfere with their right to vote can face up to a year in prison under the federal law against voter intimidation. And such intimidation can take many forms.

"It's a lot easier to explain what it is by general examples, because it's pretty amorphous," said Sophia Lin Lakin, a lawyer with the American Civil Liberties Union's Voting Rights Project. "There's not a lot of specific case law around this."

According to Ms. Lakin, intimidation can include aggressive questioning about people's qualifications to vote, including their citizenship status, criminal record or residency requirements.

Spreading false information or posing as an election official can also cross the line, she said, as can unreasonable requests for forms of identification that aren't required by law.

Intimidation can also include "questioning, challenging, photographing or videotaping" a person at a polling site, "especially under the guise of uncovering illegal voting," according to the office of the United States attorney in Arizona.

WHO IS SUSCEPTIBLE?

Voting rights advocates worry that certain groups are more likely than others to face intimidation.

Nonnative English speakers, for example, are frequently reported by people who prejudiciously assume them to be noncitizens, Ms. Lakin said. Such voters are allowed to bring translators into the voting booth as long as the translators do not employ the voters or represent them in a union.

Voters in jurisdictions with close races may also be more likely to encounter intimidation, she said. That goes as well for people of color, particularly those in areas with a history of intimidation and discrimination against nonwhite voters.

WHO CAN CHALLENGE A VOTER'S QUALIFICATIONS?

Although intimidation is prohibited, voters may still find their qualifications challenged by certified poll monitors in some states.

The monitors are typically allowed inside the polling place, but their presence is often regulated with rules governing their training, numbers and authority, according to the A.C.L.U. In many states, they may inspect polling books and challenge the qualifications of voters, but with limits.

The monitors are usually kept at a distance from the voting booth and are not allowed to interact directly with voters.

More generally, nearly every state empowers private citizens to challenge voter eligibility on or before Election Day, according to the Brennan Center for Justice at the New York University School of Law.

WHAT SHOULD YOU DO IF YOUR ELIGIBILITY IS CHALLENGED?

In many states, voters whose qualifications are challenged may still cast regular ballots if they give a sworn statement to a poll worker that they meet the qualifications, according to the A.C.L.U. In virtually all cases, voters may also request a provisional ballot.

HOW SHOULD YOU DEAL WITH INTIMIDATION IF IT OCCURS?

Anyone threatened with violence should call 911. Poll workers, the local authorities and local and state election officials may also be able to help immediately address intimidation, provided they are not culpable themselves.

While the federal government is not the ally of voting rights advocates that it was during the Obama administration, individuals may report intimidation by filing voting complaints with the Justice Department's Civil Rights Division by calling 800-253-3931, emailing voting.section@usdoj.gov or by submitting an online form. The Justice Department is also proactively monitoring elections in 35 jurisdictions in 19 states.

Voters can also report intimidation and get advice from a series of numbers associated with the nonpartisan Election Protection coalition. The main number, 866-OUR-VOTE, is administered by the Lawyers' Committee for Civil Rights Under Law. The coalition also has lines available for Spanish-speaking, Arabic-speaking and Asian-American voters.

A Poll Tax by Another Name

OPINION | BY RONALD J. KROTOSZYNSKI JR. | NOV. 14, 2016

TUSCALOOSA, ALA. — Many people, of all partisan stripes, are still wondering, "How did this happen?" The fact is that a very small difference in net votes — around 100,000 votes in Michigan, Pennsylvania and Wisconsin — would have turned Hillary Clinton's popular vote victory into an Electoral College victory as well. As people try to process what happened on Election Day, we need to consider carefully whether the difficulty of voting in our nation's urban centers, in places like Detroit, Milwaukee and Philadelphia, might have played a decisive role.

This isn't merely idle speculation. Professors Charles Stewart III, of M.I.T., and Stephen Ansolabehere, of Harvard, estimate that long lines at the polls discouraged between 500,000 and 700,000 would-be voters from casting ballots in the 2012 general election. This year, long lines, some of them a half-mile long in Cincinnati, snaked outside too many urban polling places. In Brooklyn, some voters had to wait almost three hours to vote because of unreliable voting machines.

This is hardly a new problem; reports of excessive waiting times to vote also arose in the 2004, 2008 and 2012 general elections. However, this is probably the first presidential election in which discouraged nonvoters might have determined the outcome.

No citizen should have to wait for hours to exercise the fundamental right to vote; would-be voters shouldn't be forced to choose between significant lost work time (and hence pay) and voting. Yet this is precisely the choice confronting a significant number of urban voters.

The investment of time required to vote clearly constitutes a significant disincentive to voting — a kind of modern-day poll tax. The fact that it seems to happen more often in urban and lower-income areas only underlines the need for a strong federal response.

People in line to vote in Austin, Tex., on election day.

It's difficult to know with confidence whether shorter wait times in urban precincts in Michigan, Pennsylvania and Wisconsin would have resulted in a different president-elect. In part, this is because, as the Government Accountability Office has found, 78 percent of jurisdictions don't even bother to collect data on waiting times. Even with the limited data available, however, the G.A.O. found that the polling places with the longest reported waiting times are mostly located in urban locations with "higher proportions of residents who are non-white and speak English as a second language."

For me, this is personal. My 72-year-old father lives and votes in a predominantly African-American precinct in Moss Point, Miss. Although he knew that his vote would probably not make a difference, he waited for over an hour in a line stretching down the block.

But how many people made a different choice on Tuesday? For many of them, it was not even a real choice. As between voting and paying the rent, many citizens were simply unable to spend an hour or more queuing to vote. The outcome of a presidential election should not potentially turn on votes not cast out of a combination of frustration and economic necessity.

We amended the Constitution to abolish poll taxes for federal elections in 1964, and two years later the Supreme Court extended this principle to state and local elections. "Voter qualifications have no relation to wealth nor to paying or not paying this or any other tax," the court ruled. When a voter has to wait in line for hours in order to vote, that's effectively a form of poll tax.

In an ideal world, Congress would establish a maximum mean wait time for voting in federal elections and require all jurisdictions to meet the national standard. Moreover, the wait times within a given jurisdiction should be more or less equal.

Alternatively, given Bush v. Gore's application of equal-protection principles to counting votes, it would be possible for the federal courts, as a matter of equal-protection doctrine, to force states to reduce the gross disparities in the time required to vote. If a state does not want to open more precincts or use more voting machines in high-population precincts to equalize wait times, it could follow the lead of states like Colorado, Oregon and Washington, all of which use vote-by-mail systems that reduce the temporal poll tax to zero.

At the very least, one person, one vote means that in a participatory democracy, the temporal burden of voting should be evenly distributed among all citizens. In the United States today, it is not.

RONALD J. KROTOSZYNSKI JR. is a professor of law at the University of Alabama.

400,000 New Yorkers Were Told Their Voter Registrations Were Inactive. Oops.

BY WILLIAM NEUMAN | OCT. 16, 2018

HUNDREDS OF THOUSANDS of New Yorkers got a letter in recent days warning them of possible problems with their voter registration — sowing confusion and leading many to think the letter was part of a voter suppression scheme.

The letter was actually an initiative by Mayor Bill de Blasio to encourage voting — one of the few new initiatives of his second term.

"You were marked as an inactive voter by the New York City Board of Elections," the letter said, "but you may still be eligible to vote in the upcoming election."

It went on to say that inactive voters had until Wednesday to rectify their status by submitting an address-confirmation notice to the Board of Elections or by filling out a new voter registration form.

Many of the people who got the letter, however, were regular voters whose registrations were not inactive. They reacted with alarm and suspicion, saying the letter was confusing and that it was unclear who had sent it.

Jessica Apgar, 40, of Manhattan, had just voted in the primary election last month, so she was suspicious when she received the letter on Monday. She checked the Board of Elections website and saw that it listed her as an active voter.

Then she took to Twitter to inquire if others "got this mistake." She worried that others might get the letter and be discouraged from voting.

"It wasn't just panic from my voting rights, it was panic that other people were going to take this and not look into it and maybe just say, 'Oh well, I just won't vote.' "

The Board of Elections replied, confirming her active status and distancing itself from the letter.

"This letter was created by an outside entity," the board said in a Twitter post. "Not sure where they got their info from."

Mr. de Blasio, who has criticized the Board of Elections in the past for incorrectly purging voters from the rolls and for inefficiency, announced in August that the city would conduct "extensive, nonpartisan outreach to more than 561,000 inactive voters to ensure that they remain registered and to avoid any possibility of removing eligible voters from voter rolls."

"The Board of Elections has not done a good enough job at communicating with voters," Mr. de Blasio said at the time on NY1. "The City of New York is going to do that now more and more." He added that the city had purchased a list of inactive voters that it was using to identify who to reach out to.

On Tuesday, the mayor's office said that the list came from Civis Analytics, a business and political consultant. Such companies typically buy raw voter data from elections boards and sort and analyze it for their clients.

Efforts to reach Civis officials were unsuccessful. And the mayor's office sought to blame the Board of Elections on Tuesday.

"It has come to our attention that a very small group of active voters may have received inaccurate letters from the city identifying them as inactive voters," the mayor's press secretary, Eric F. Phillips, said in a statement. "We're working to get to the bottom of why the mailing list used, which originated with the city Board of Elections, seems to have led to this error."

He acknowledged that people who got the letter might be "understandably confused" and encouraged them to check their registration status online. Raul Contreras, a mayoral spokesman, said that the letter was sent to more than 400,000 people.

The mayor's office did not explain why the letter went out so close to the apparent deadline for inactive voters to change their status.

It was also not clear whether the mayor's newly appointed chief democracy officer, Ayirini Fonseca-Sabune, was involved in drafting and sending the letter. Mr. de Blasio announced in February that he was creating the position so someone could lead his efforts to improve the city's voting system and encourage more New Yorkers to vote and participate in politics; Ms. Fonseca-Sabune was not named to the post until this month.

Michael Ryan, the executive director of the New York City Board of Elections, said on Tuesday that the board had received about 1,100 calls from people inquiring about the letter.

"We were not consulted with respect to the contents of the letter; we were not notified that the letter was going out," Mr. Ryan said.

"Let's be clear, a private vendor purchased this list," he said. "What they do with the data once it's in their hands is their business, so how they crafted a list of 400,000 people is anybody's guess."

Voters can be listed as inactive if mail sent to them is returned to the Board of Elections by the post office because it could not be delivered. Inactive voters are still registered and can vote on Election Day on Nov. 6 with an affidavit ballot.

Why Deep Blue New York Is 'Voter Suppression Land'

BY VIVIAN WANG | DEC. 19, 2018

IN 2016, WHEN the governor of Ohio was asked why he had signed a bill to limit early voting, he had a simple retort: He pointed to another state that had no early voting at all.

When North Carolina's governor was sued for cutting early voting in his own state, his lawyers cited that same state as rebuttal.

In each case, the state in question was New York. Deep blue, liberal-ideal New York.

Despite its reputation for sterling progressivism, New York has some of the most restrictive election laws in the nation. It is one of just 12 states without early voting. No other state holds its federal and state primary elections on different days. Voters who want to change their party affiliation must do so more than a year before the election, a rule that famously left Ivanka Trump unable to vote for her father in the 2016 Republican primary.

"New Yorkers would be aghast if anyone accused New York of voter suppression," said Donna Lieberman, executive director of the New York Civil Liberties Union. But, she said, "the antiquated nature of our laws and the failure to enact any common-sense reforms for years puts us kind of in voter suppression land."

That failure may finally end next year, now that Democrats have captured the State Senate, giving the party control of both legislative chambers and the governor's seat for the first time in a decade.

On Monday, Gov. Andrew M. Cuomo unveiled a lengthy list of election reforms, promising to make them his priorities for the first 100 days of the new year. The list included early voting, automatic voter registration, vote-by-mail and a merging of the dates of the federal and state primary elections.

KARSTEN MORAN FOR THE NEW YORK TIMES

Despite its reputation for progressivism, New York has some of the most restrictive election laws in the nation. Gov. Andrew Cuomo has vowed to change that next year.

"The federal government is working to disenfranchise voters. We have to do the exact opposite and improve our democracy," Mr. Cuomo, a Democrat, said in a speech. "Let's make a real statement about the importance of voting, and let's make Election Day a state holiday and say to people, 'Get out and vote.'"

The governor also threw his support behind an overhaul of campaign finance laws, including banning all corporate contributions and closing the so-called L.L.C. loophole, which allows real estate moguls and others to donate unlimited amounts to candidates.

Mr. Cuomo and Democrats in both legislative chambers have pushed bills to overhaul the state's elections for years, but the Republican-controlled Senate had consistently refused to call them to the floor for a vote, despite a declared desire to lift New York's abysmal voter turnout rates. Low turnout among Democrats has historically helped Republicans overcome their enrollment disad-

124 VOTER SUPPRESSION

vantage. Critics have also cited concerns about the cost of early voting.

Democrats have promised that their long-stalled initiatives will finally become law.

"Our priorities will involve many of the bills that the Assembly has passed time and again," said Assemblyman Charles Lavine, who chairs the chamber's elections committee.

But even the most ardent backers acknowledged political and logistical obstacles.

Not only Republicans are to blame for the inertia of voting reform in New York, according to Wendy Weiser, the director of the Democracy Program at New York University's Brennan Center for Justice. Machine politics and the advantages of incumbency make many politicians wary of changing the system.

"Elected officials often oppose changes to the electoral system in which they were elected," Ms. Weiser said. "It's the incumbency protection agency: 'It worked for me, it must be a good system.' "

Mr. Lavine said he expected early voting and merging primaries to pass immediately, but he was more reserved on the prospects of public financing of campaigns or a ban on corporate money; he said the Assembly would give those ideas "great consideration."

"It's not that I anticipate blowback in the classic sense," he said of the corporate money proposal. "But this is something that is going to require a lot of discussion. And both Democratic conferences, in the Senate and the Assembly, have to listen to the concerns of each of their members."

Mr. Cuomo, who has been a vocal supporter of election reform — he has repeatedly included measures such as public financing and closing the L.L.C. loophole in his executive budgets — has also reaped the benefits of its failure, raising tens of millions of dollars for his formidable war chest in part by taking advantage of the loophole.

There may be administrative tangles as well. Two popular proposed reforms — Election Day voter registration and mail-in voting — would require a constitutional amendment, which would have to be passed in two consecutive legislative sessions and then ratified by voters, Ms. Weiser said. Rolling out early voting and automatic voter registration, while they could become law immediately, would require money and infrastructure.

But Ms. Weiser added that studies have indicated that automatic registration would pay for itself within one or two election cycles, and that early voting would provide immeasurable convenience, allowing officials to avert the kind of Election Day snafus that paralyzed much of New York City this year.

Still, advocates acknowledged that legislators' whims were unpredictable, and that the political obstacles could loom far larger than the logistical ones. But they also said that the visibility of many officials' prior statements would make it politically dangerous for them to backtrack.

"Nothing is 100 percent guaranteed in Albany," said Susan Lerner, the executive director of Common Cause New York, a government reform group. But she added: "I think it would be very very difficult for people who were elected on the promise that they were going to heed the voice of the voter, to then turn around and just have it be old-fashioned Albany business as usual."

Of course, that is the argument of many other advocates, on many other issues, all of whom are counting on the newly remade government to unleash their own long-stymied legislation. And Albany has disappointed many a lobbyist and activist before.

But Ms. Weiser suggested that the dashing of these hopes — so long-held and in many ways so common-sense — would have special resonance.

"I do think it would be a travesty if New York is unable to get this done," she said. "Not just a missed opportunity, but I think it would be a setback, at a point when the public is so clearly demanding it."

Tennessee Advances Bill That Could Make It Harder to Register New Voters

BY MATT STEVENS | APRIL 16, 2019

TENNESSEE LAWMAKERS PASSED a bill through the state House on Monday that would fine community groups that submit incomplete voter-registration applications, an unusual move that the bill's opponents have denounced as voter suppression.

Protesters swarmed the State Capitol to speak out against the Republican-backed bill, which has drawn condemnation from voting rights advocates and Democratic lawmakers, who say it would discriminate against minority voters in a state where overall turnout is already abysmal.

"It's clearly intended to have a chilling effect on voting efforts across Tennessee," John Ray Clemmons, a Democratic state representative, said of the bill.

Tens of thousands of new black and Latino voters were registered in Tennessee in the run-up to the 2018 midterm elections, but thousands of applications in Shelby County were disqualified by state election officials for what critics say were frivolous reasons. Republicans have cited the dispute as rationale for passing the legislation.

"We want every eligible Tennessean to vote, and voter registration must be done responsibly and in a manner that does not compromise the security or integrity of elections," said Tre Hargett, the Republican secretary of state, on Tuesday.

Republicans maintain a supermajority in both the state House and Senate. A spokesman for Tennessee's House Republican Caucus said the Senate could consider its version of the bill within a matter of days.

The governor, Bill Lee, is a first-term Republican who was elected in November; he was noncommittal when asked about the legislation Monday, according to The Associated Press. A spokeswoman for Mr. Lee did not return a request for comment.

But the bill's opponents, including Mr. Clemmons, say they expect it to be signed into law. It could then face legal challenges.

"We're prepared to keep fighting," said Charlane Oliver, a co-founder of the Equity Alliance, a Tennessee-based nonprofit that advocates for African-Americans to get involved in the civic process.

The Tennessee proposal is just the latest of a flurry of measures across the country that have made it harder to vote. Since 2010, 25 states — from Arizona to New Hampshire — have imposed strict photo identification requirements, cut back on early voting periods or imposed other restrictions, according to The Brennan Center for Justice, a nonpartisan law and policy institute based in New York.

In 2018 alone, at least a half-dozen states enacted new restrictions, the center said.

Myrna Pérez, who leads the Brennan Center's Voting Rights and Elections Project, said that states have sometimes taken steps to regulate community groups and nonprofit organizations that are seeking to register voters.

But she said she found the Tennessee legislation concerning because it would impose so many rules at once, and because there appeared to be no allegation that those driving the registration efforts had been anything other than sloppy.

"I am entirely sympathetic to the claims that are being made that this is an attempt to stifle and chill voter registration drives, and it may have the impact of doing so," she said.

The bill would apply to people or organizations who conduct registration drives, seek to collect 100 or more voter registration forms and pay individuals to collect the forms. Officials say it would not apply to individuals or organizations who collect forms using only unpaid volunteers.

It would impose civil penalties on those who file 100 or more "deficient" voter registration applications, starting at $150 in each county where a violation occurred. Under the bill, any person or group that filed more than 500 faulty applications could be fined up to $10,000.

In addition, it would make it a Class A misdemeanor to establish a minimum number of registration forms for workers to collect.

Ms. Oliver said the bill was an attempt to place the burden of processing applications on community groups rather than on the government.

"It's totally wrong to penalize people for doing one of the most democratic acts in this nation — registering voters," she said.

Wisconsin Judge Says State Must Purge 200,000 Voter Registrations

BY MONICA DAVEY AND MITCH SMITH | DEC. 13, 2019

The decision, which was derided by Democrats, comes in a fight to win Wisconsin in the 2020 presidential election.

THREE YEARS AGO, fewer than 23,000 votes handed Donald J. Trump a crucial victory in Wisconsin, a state that many had assumed would again be won by the Democratic candidate. The takeaway for 2020 in a state that was now seen as a key prize: Every last vote would matter.

On Friday, far more Wisconsin voters — some 200,000 — were ordered dropped from the state's voting rolls in a court ruling that was sending political operatives and officials scrambling.

"This would create chaos to do this now," Karla Keckhaver, a lawyer defending the Wisconsin Elections Commission, told the judge who issued the ruling to purge thousands of the state's voters from the rolls.

The ruling, by Judge Paul V. Malloy of the Ozaukee County Circuit Court, grew out of a legal fight over what should come of thousands of voters who were sent letters by state election officials because they were believed to have moved.

Those who did not respond to the letters were to be removed from the voting rolls, but not until 2021, state officials had indicated. But a conservative group, the Wisconsin Institute for Law & Liberty, filed a lawsuit, saying that election officials were required to remove names more rapidly.

Judge Malloy concurred.

"I don't want to see anybody deactivated, but I don't write the legislation," Judge Malloy said as he gave his ruling from the bench on Friday.

He discussed a hypothetical situation in which a close election might be tipped by an improperly registered voter. "If somebody in one of these close elections were to tie, and some voters voted that shouldn't have been in that district because their registration wasn't correct, you really can't undo that," Judge Malloy said.

"This case is about whether a state agency can ignore clearly written state law," said Rick Esenberg, president of the Wisconsin Institute for Law & Liberty. "Today's court order requires the Wisconsin Elections Commission to follow state law, and we look forward to making the case that they must continue to follow state law."

Wisconsin Democrats, though, saw the decision as about something far different than following housekeeping rules when it comes to voter rolls. They said conservatives were merely searching for ways to remove Democratic voters in an effort to boost the Republicans' chances in 2020.

Ben Wikler, the chairman of the Democratic Party of Wisconsin, said the lawsuit was the "product of a right-wing legal and political strategy to prevent eligible voters from voting." He added, "It should be a concern to anyone who believes in the core idea of democracy."

Gov. Tony Evers, a Democrat who was elected by fewer than 30,000 votes last year, tweeted, "This move pushed by Republicans to remove 200,000 Wisconsinites from the voter rolls is just another attempt at overriding the will of the people and stifling the democratic process."

When The Milwaukee Journal Sentinel analyzed the list of voters that were believed to have moved, it found that about 55 percent of them lived in municipalities that Hillary Clinton carried in the 2016 election. The highest concentrations were mostly in college towns and the state's two largest cities, Milwaukee and Madison.

State election officials said they were analyzing the judge's ruling and sorting through what to do next. An appeal seemed likely.

In Wisconsin, where 3.3 million people are registered to cast ballots, voters who are purged from the rolls can choose to register again, including on Election Day.

MONICA DAVEY is the Chicago bureau chief, covering the Midwest. She joined The Times in 2003. She previously worked at The Chicago Tribune, and wrote for the St. Petersburg (Fla.) Times, the Roanoke Times and others.

MITCH SMITH covers the Midwest and the Great Plains. Since joining The Times in 2014, he has written extensively about gun violence, oil pipelines, state-level politics and the national debate over police tactics. He is based in Chicago.

Federal Judge Backs Georgia's Purge of Nearly 100,000 Voters

BY ELISHA BROWN | DEC. 27, 2019

A FEDERAL JUDGE on Friday backed Georgia's removal of nearly 100,000 names from the state's voter rolls.

The decision comes as state officials face accusations of voter suppression, particularly against black and low-income voters. Scrutiny of voting rights in Georgia has been heightened since the governor's race in 2018 brought long lines at polling sites and criticism of outdated voting machines.

In the ruling, the judge, Steve C. Jones, said the lead plaintiff, Fair Fight Action, a voting rights advocacy organization, did not prove that the Georgia secretary of state's decision to cancel the voter registration status of inactive voters violated the United States Constitution.

The judge, an appointee of former President Obama, also ordered the secretary of state to make "diligent and reasonable efforts" through its website and news releases to inform residents about registration, especially residents that have until Monday to re-register to vote ahead of a special election in January for a seat in the state's House of Representatives.

In October, Georgia officials announced plans to remove more than 300,000 names from its lists of voters. About 100,000 had moved to a different county or state and about 80,000 had mail that was classified as undeliverable.

Fair Fight Action argued against the removal of about 120,000 voters from the state's rolls and the state restored about 22,000 names to the voting rolls.

According to court documents, Fair Fight Action argued that the state was disenfranchising voters after a name was purged because of the state's "use it or lose it" rule, which bumps from the rolls voters who had not voted in the past several elections.

Voters in Savannah, Ga., during the 2018 mid-term elections. A federal judge on Friday sided with the state's removal of nearly 100,000 voters from the rolls.

In 2019, Gov. Brian Kemp signed a bill into law requiring the secretary of state to wait five years before removing inactive voters. Previously, the state was allowed to remove names from rolls if there was no contact with a voter for three years.

"Our efforts to protect Georgia voters have already resulted in approximately 26,500 voters remaining on the rolls who would have otherwise been purged, and the state is now required to take additional steps to notify purged voters as a result of our litigation," Lauren Groh-Wargo, Fair Fight Action's chief executive, said in a statement.

Brad Raffensperger, Georgia's secretary of state, said in a statement that the ruling "upheld Georgia's decision to continue to maintain clean voter rolls."

"Despite activists efforts and lawsuits that only waste taxpayer dollars, Georgia is continuing to ensure every eligible voter can vote and voter lists remain accurate," he said.

Fair Fight Action was founded by Stacey Abrams, the Democrat who narrowly lost the race for governor in 2018 to Mr. Kemp, Georgia's former secretary of state. In March, the House Oversight and Reform Committee began an investigation into voter suppression in the state.

The ruling in Georgia comes amid voter restrictions and purges elsewhere in the country.

A legal notice filed on Thursday showed that a federal judge in North Carolina planned to block a new voter identification law that critics had said would deter black and Latino residents from voting. The state N.A.A.C.P. had sued and sought an injunction against the law.

The judge, Loretta C. Biggs, who was also an Obama administration appointee, noted that the state Board of Elections said it planned a large statewide mailing to educate voters about the law on Tuesday. She said she would grant the plaintiffs' request for an injunction and would formally block the requirement, which was scheduled to begin in 2020.

Unless the preliminary injunction is successfully appealed, the requirement will be halted until the lawsuit is resolved.

And this month, a Wisconsin judge ruled that 200,000 names should be removed from the voter rolls. Wisconsin has become a battleground state ahead of the 2020 presidential election.

KAREN ZRAICK contributed reporting. **JACK BEGG** contributed research.

CHAPTER 4

The 2018 Georgia Governor's Race

In 2018, the election for governor of Georgia was a case study in voter suppression. Georgia's secretary of state, Republican candidate Brian Kemp, stalled the registrations of 53,000 voters, most of whom were African-American. Democratic candidate Stacey Abrams argued that Kemp's actions were a transparent attempt to suppress her candidacy, given that black voters in Georgia are much more likely to vote for a Democrat. Abrams ultimately lost the election by only about 55,000 votes. In the wake of her loss, she launched an organization to support voting rights.

Georgia County Rejects Plan to Close 7 Polling Places in Majority-Black Area

BY RICHARD FAUSSET | AUG. 23, 2018

CUTHBERT, GA. — The consultant, a white man, came to the mainly black Randolph County in rural southern Georgia and recommended that it eliminate seven of its nine polling places. He said the move would save the county money. He said the polling places had disability compliance issues.

But many people in the county assumed a more sinister motive, especially with the state in the midst of a hotly contested election for governor. It pits a Democrat who would be Georgia's first black chief executive against a white Republican who has been called a "master of voter suppression" by his political opponents.

"I think it was an effort to suppress the vote," Bobby Jenkins, 66, a retired Randolph County school superintendent, said after a meeting on Wednesday where local residents complained that African-Americans in poor rural areas would be left having to drive long distances to vote. "This is one typical strategy in the Republican playbooks."

The Randolph County plan was rejected Friday morning on a 2-0 vote by the county's board of elections. The two members, a black woman and a white man, voted hastily and without comment, leaving a press statement that acknowledged the interest from the news media, residents and civil rights groups.

"The interest and concern shown has been overwhelming, and it is an encouraging reminder that protecting the right to vote remains a fundamental American principle," it said.

But some say it may not be the last flash point over voting access in Georgia.

Mistrust and bad blood permeate what is shaping up to be a historic election for governor. In the years leading up to the showdown between Brian Kemp, the Republican secretary of state, and Stacey Abrams, the Democratic former state House minority leader, Georgia has been caught up in one controversy after another, locally and statewide, over election integrity, voting access and race.

The American Civil Liberties Union has been sending its members to observe meetings of other local election commissions across the state, and to watch for similar proposals that could curtail voter access, according to Andrea Young, the executive director of the group's Georgia chapter.

"We sort of anticipated a bit of what's happening in Randolph County, that there might be efforts to close polls ahead of this election," Ms. Young said.

The two candidates, Mr. Kemp and Ms. Abrams, have squared off over voting rights before. As secretary of state, Mr. Kemp has overseen Georgia's elections since 2010. He is a fervent fan of President Trump, who has made numerous baseless claims about voter fraud.

For years, Mr. Kemp's critics in Georgia, including Ms. Abrams, have accused him of supporting policies that adversely affect minority voters and contravene federal law. They also say he has conducted overzealous investigations of voter registration groups, including one founded by Ms. Abrams. The state's Democratic Party has called on him to resign his current office in order to ensure an impartial election.

Mr. Kemp has insisted that he had nothing to do with the plan to close polling places in Randolph County, and wrote to the county advising it not to go ahead with the plan.

Unfettered access to the polls for minority voters is vital to Ms. Abrams's election campaign. She has adopted a strategy that relies less on wooing conservative white Democrats in the countryside, as her party has done in the past, and more on a surge of highly motivated liberals and nonwhite voters, in an increasingly diverse state: By 2030, non-Hispanic whites are expected to make up less than half the population.

For decades, the federal government acted as a referee on voting issues in the Deep South under the Voting Rights Act of 1965. But the Supreme Court sharply curtailed federal oversight in a 2013 decision.

Before that ruling, a polling-place consolidation proposal like the one that has rocked Randolph County would almost certainly have been subject to preclearance review by the Justice Department, with the county obliged to show that it would not disproportionately disadvantage minority voters.

Mike Malone, an independent election consultant who recommended the polling-place closings, had been hired by the county earlier this year to help it with voting logistics after the county elections superintendent resigned.

In community meetings last week, Mr. Malone said that the seven polling places were not heavily used — just 12 people voted at one of them in a recent election — and that some did not comply with the Americans With Disabilities Act.

But when the word got out about his proposal, it struck many as drastic. The civil liberties union wrote to the county that the plan would make it "disproportionately harder" for black voters to cast a ballot. The Lawyers' Committee for Civil Rights Under Law threatened to sue, arguing that closing the polling places over accessibility made little sense.

"Forcing elderly, disabled, and other persons with mobility issues to travel lengthy distances to vote is out of place with the purported goal of A.D.A. compliance," its lawyers wrote to the county.

As Friday's vote neared, it became difficult to find anyone, Democrat or Republican, who supported the proposal. On Wednesday, the county attorney sent a letter terminating the county's contract with Mr. Malone.

Suspicion also spread that Mr. Kemp was somehow behind the recommendation — a claim he adamantly denies.

A spokeswoman for the secretary of state's office, Candice Broce, said that an official in her office had recommended Mr. Malone to the county as a qualified election expert, but that he was one of several consultants mentioned.

In public meetings, Mr. Malone has shown a slide saying that a policy of consolidating polling places "has come highly recommended by the secretary of state." But Ms. Broce said that Mr. Kemp's office urged the county to abandon Mr. Malone's plan.

"They need to focus on preparing for a secure, accessible, and fair election in November," she said. "Our position on this issue is crystal clear."

Some black Georgia residents say they are primed to be skeptical of Republican motives, given the repeated efforts by Republican officials to limit voting access in the name of efficiency or fraud prevention.

Republican state lawmakers introduced a bill earlier this year to curtail early voting on Sundays, when many black Christian congregations conduct "Souls to the Polls" voting drives. The legislation died after being opposed by the Rev. Raphael Warnock, senior pastor at the Atlanta church where Dr. Martin Luther King Jr. once preached.

There have been local disputes in counties across the state over polling-place consolidation and other issues. But Mr. Kemp is the public official who has come in for the most criticism from Georgia liberals and voting-rights activists, who say he has been aggressive in trying to suppress minority voting.

In 2014, he was recorded encouraging a Republican group to register like-minded voters, and warning them that Democrats were "working hard" to register "all these minority voters that are out there and others that are sitting on the sidelines."

Mr. Kemp's supporters maintain that he is a champion of ballot access, noting that record numbers of votes were cast on his watch in 2016 and that the rejection rate for voter registrations that year were ninth-lowest in the country.

"If he's the master of voter suppression, he's doing a terrible job of it," Ms. Broce said.

Even so, civil rights groups have engaged with Mr. Kemp over a number of policies. They forced him to change voter registration deadlines that contravened federal law, and got him to change registration forms that erroneously told new voters that they had to mail in documents proving their name and address.

Mr. Kemp was also sued over a system that begins a process of purging voters from the rolls if they do not vote for three consecutive years, though in June the Supreme Court upheld a similar system in Ohio.

Civil rights groups are currently criticizing Mr. Kemp over a law that they call "no match, no vote," in which voter registrations are flagged as "pending" if a name, address or other information does not exactly match what is in the state drivers' license database or Social Security records, down to the letter. If the voter does not correct the discrepancy, he or she is dropped from the rolls after 26 months.

The Lawyers' Committee said the process has an "extraordinarily high error rate" and that minority voters are heavily affected.

Mr. Kemp said in a statement last month that the state law was legal and that a similar law in Florida was upheld in federal court. "Not a single voter whose status is pending for failure to verify will get rejected this election cycle," he said.

He also suggested that complaints about the law were politically motivated. "Nov. 6, 2018, is right around the corner, which means it's high time for another frivolous lawsuit from liberal activist groups," he said.

His office has also attracted criticism for vigorous investigations of potential voter fraud that some advocates say is overkill. In 2010, in an incident chronicled by The Atlanta Journal-Constitution, his office participated in a sweeping investigation in Brooks County, Ga., where black candidates had just won a majority on the local school board after an organized absentee-ballot drive.

A dozen organizers were indicted on various election-law charges. None were convicted: One died before trial, one was tried and acquitted, and the remaining cases were dropped in 2014.

A two-and-a-half-year investigation of an Asian-American rights group's voter registration activities by Mr. Kemp's office ended in 2015 without finding any violations, according to The New Republic. Helen Ho, a lawyer who founded the group, said in an interview on Thursday that the whole thing seemed intended to intimidate the group.

In 2014, Mr. Kemp's office began an investigation into a minority-focused voter registration group that Ms. Abrams founded, the New Georgia Project. The inquiry was prompted by complaints from 16 counties that included suspicions that canvassers may have been acting illegally and submitting falsified documents.

The New Georgia Project responded with a lawsuit accusing state and local elections officials of failing to properly process more than 40,000 voter applications, but a Georgia judge dismissed the case one week before the November 2014 elections.

The investigation ended with the discovery of 53 fraudulent voter applications. Fourteen canvassers were referred to the state attorney general's office, where they may face fines as part of what the office calls a "civil administrative matter."

No concrete evidence of ulterior motives has emerged in the Randolph County polling-place controversy. But the Abrams campaign has seized on it as a leading campaign theme just the same. As of Friday morning, a Twitter message about it was pinned at the top of her social media account.

"Efforts to suppress the vote & depress voter turnout are alive & well in Georgia," it read.

Showdown in Georgia
Governor's Race Reflects a Larger Fight Over Voting Rights

BY ASTEAD W. HERNDON AND TRIP GABRIEL | OCT. 15, 2018

ATLANTA — Reports that tens of thousands of Georgia voters, predominantly African-Americans, were placed on a list for further scrutiny have exploded into the Georgia governor's race, leading to bitter exchanges between the candidates and leaving many residents uncertain what to expect as the state began early voting Monday.

The uproar over voting seems almost an inevitable development in the race, which pits two candidates on opposite sides of the nation's voting wars who have battled with one another over access to the polls for years.

Stacey Abrams, the Democrat, who is hoping to be the nation's first black female governor, forged her political profile through a group she founded that in the last five years has registered thousands of new minority voters. Her opponent Brian Kemp, Georgia's secretary of state since 2010, has advanced strict voting rules that he says are needed to combat fraud, but which critics call a form of voter suppression directed at precisely the new voters Ms. Abrams is aiming to bring to the polls.

Their race is the latest example of how contentious and far-reaching voting issues have become in American politics, where once largely nonpartisan issues have been weaponized to gain an edge.

Ms. Abrams on Sunday repeated calls for Mr. Kemp to resign as the state's top elections official to avoid a conflict of interest. She accused him of disenfranchising minorities for years, including his office's latest effort, suspending the processing of 53,000 voter registrations, mainly African-Americans. It fits "a pattern of behavior where he tries to tilt the playing field in his favor," Ms. Abrams said on NBC's "Meet the Press."

Mr. Kemp told the Valdosta Daily Times Sunday that it was a "politically motivated, manufactured story," made up by his opponent to drum up Democratic turnout. Everyone on the suspended list will be able to cast a ballot, he said. And he leveled an incendiary charge of his own at Ms. Abrams: that she wants noncitizens' votes to count. "She wants illegals to vote in Georgia," he said on Fox News on Monday.

Ms. Abrams accused Mr. Kemp of intentionally taking comments she made out of context.

As early voting began Monday, Ms. Abrams kicked off a week-long bus tour of Georgia churches and schools, with the topic of voter suppression coming up within minutes.

The current controversy began after an analysis last week by The Associated Press found that 70 percent of 53,000 new registrations currently suspended were for black Georgians.

A state law passed in 2017 at Mr. Kemp's urging requires an "exact match" between a voter's registration form and his or her government documents. A missing hyphen, or a difference between a married and a maiden name, causes a registration to be suspended.

Many of the stalled registrations were voters signed up by the New Georgia Project, Ms. Abrams's group, which has worked for years to boost minorities' registrations.

Despite being on hold, all of the 53,000 pending voters will be able to vote this year with a proper photo ID that matches their registration, said Michael McDonald, an elections law expert at the University of Florida, who was an expert witness in a lawsuit over the issue of exact-match registration.

But Ms. Abrams said uncertainty alone might cause many new voters not to show up on Election Day, especially low-propensity voters in rural areas who are not following the issue closely.

"They get a confusing letter saying there's something wrong with their registration," she said on Sunday. "And more than likely they will sit out this election. The miasma of fear that is created through voter suppression is as much about terrifying people about trying to vote as it is about actually blocking their ability to do so."

Mr. McDonald added that, absent another successful lawsuit, the 53,000 on the list will have to prove they are legally registered to vote in 2019 and the 2020 presidential race.

Experts say any impediment to voting can be enough to dissuade someone from casting a ballot.

Michelle Dehaven, a veterinarian based in Smyrna, Ga., said she learned over the summer she had been temporarily dropped from voting rolls when she visited the Department of Motor Vehicles to replace a lost driver's license. She was told she was no longer registered to vote.

"It never occurred to me it would be a problem," she said. When she called the Secretary of State's office to fix the problem, she said, the person who answered informed her, "I don't know, I can't help you."

Eventually, county election officials helped her return to the voter rolls. "I had to really fuss," Ms. Dehaven said. "I'm educated and I'm well versed in this. But it was just shocking."

The Georgia race highlights the national transformation of the office of secretary of state since the disputed 2000 election between George W. Bush and Al Gore. Once a low-visibility, uncontroversial job, focused on administering voting laws in a nonpartisan way, secretaries of state in many places have become politicized.

This year, two of the most activist-minded Republican secretaries of state are running for governor: Mr. Kemp of Georgia and Kris Kobach of Kansas, who was the face of President Trump's commission that unsuccessfully sought proof of widespread voter fraud in the 2016 election.

Both are in statistically tied races, according to polls. Should the vote on Nov. 6 be so close in either state that a recount is necessary (or, in Georgia, a runoff if no one wins a majority), the candidates would face a conflict of interest in the determination of the victor.

The issue is not academic. Mr. Kobach awoke the morning after his Republican primary in August leading an opponent, the incumbent Gov. Jeff Colyer, by just 121 votes.

At first, Mr. Kobach refused to recuse himself, as the state's chief elections official, from a potential recount, arguing that the counting would be done by local officials. Eventually, under pressure, he turned over his duties to a top deputy. No recount took place, as Mr. Kobach's lead grew to 345 and Mr. Colyer conceded.

More important than any possible role in umpiring a close election, Mr. Kemp and Mr. Kobach have for years narrowed who is eligible to vote, in ways that critics say are intended to help Republicans by suppressing votes by minorities, the poor and college students — groups that lean Democratic.

Mr. Kobach was the author of a Kansas law that required proof of citizenship to register to vote. Before it was struck down in June in federal court, the law blocked 31,000 Kansans from registering.

Despite repeated studies disproving Mr. Kobach's claims that waves of "illegal aliens" cast votes, he has not toned down his rhetoric, which plays well with the party's base.

The battle over election rules reached a boiling point in 2016, when federal courts struck down or curtailed some of the most restrictive ballot laws in North Carolina, Wisconsin, Texas and elsewhere. But Republican backers of restrictions have since found more success in cases before an increasingly conservative federal judiciary.

In North Dakota, for example, a federal court has refused to stay a state law that require voters to display ID cards with addresses. The seemingly routine requirement is aimed at Native Americans, whose culture discourages fixed addresses.

At the same time, a number of states have moved in recent years to make it easier to vote. Thirteen states have approved automatic voter registration laws, four of them this year. Utah voters will be able to register on Election Day in November for the first time, and Washington approved a state voting-rights law and preregistration for 16- and 17-year-olds.

In Georgia, Mr. Kemp has overseen the mass cancellation of 1.4 million registrations since 2012. Although federal law requires updating voter rolls by removing the dead or those who have moved, critics charge that aggressive purges have led to many eligible voters being unfairly removed. A study by the Brennan Center for Justice found that states with a history of racial discrimination, which were freed from federal oversight under a 2013 Supreme Court voting rights decision, have had significantly higher purge rates.

Mr. Kemp "has long had a reputation for over-aggressive purging, trying to make it more difficult for African-Americans to vote as part of a political strategy," said Miles S. Rapoport, a former secretary of state of Connecticut, who is senior fellow at the Harvard Kennedy School.

ASTEAD W. HERNDON reported from Atlanta, and **TRIP GABRIEL** from New York. **MAGGIE ASTOR** contributed reporting from New York, and **MICHAEL WINES** from Washington.

Georgia Voting Begins Amid Accusations of Voter Suppression

BY ASTEAD W. HERNDON | OCT. 19, 2018

MARIETTA, GA. — Wim Laven arrived to his polling location in Atlanta's northern suburbs this week unsure what to make of recent allegations of voter difficulties at the ballot box. Then he waited two hours in the Georgia sun; saw one person in the line treated for heat exhaustion; and watched a second collapse, receive help from paramedics, yet refuse to be taken to the hospital — so he could remain in line and cast his ballot.

Mr. Laven is now a believer.

"I have a hard time imaging this is anything but an intentional effort," said Mr. Laven, who teaches political science at Kennesaw State University. "I can't imagine this is just pure incompetence. Everyone knew how serious people have been around here about getting out the vote."

As Georgians cast their first in-person ballots on Monday in the state's fiercely contested gubernatorial election, what were once hypothetical fears about the state's inability to handle what could be a record turnout for a nonpresidential election may be becoming reality.

Vote totals have increased almost 200 percent at the same point since the last gubernatorial election, according to the independent tracker Georgia Votes, but many worry the state has either failed to adequately prepare for such increased interest or Republican state officials have intentionally mounted barriers to dissuade communities of likely Democratic residents from voting.

Some of the concerns reflect longstanding complaints, such as reduced polling locations, confusion among election workers, and outdated voting machines which may soon be deemed illegal. Since 2012, more than 200 local voting precincts have been closed across the state of Georgia, which amount to about 8 percent of the state's total polling places.

While canvassing in Lilburn, Ga., with the group Care in Action, Sanaa Lahgazi, left, spoke with Kimberly Edwards, who said her husband had been purged from the voter rolls.

But there are also allegations of intentional voter suppression, which has become a central issue in the governor's race. A recent report by The Associated Press detailed how Georgia Secretary of State Brian Kemp, who is also the Republican nominee for governor, had stalled more than 50,000 voter registrations of disproportionately black voters because of alleged problems with their voting registration information.

Mr. Kemp has denied allegations of intentional voter suppression and said that all persons on that list can still vote on Election Day, if they have the proper identification. Still, the back-and-forth has ignited nervousness and confusion among supporters of Stacey Abrams, the Democratic gubernatorial nominee, who is seeking to become the first black female governor.

The Democratic Party of Georgia, through a spokesman, said its voter protection hotline has received about 300 calls a day since early voting began.

"It's absolutely crazy," said Kimberly Edwards, 37, who said she recently learned her husband had been purged from voting rolls after skipping the 2016 election. She found out when a canvasser knocked on her door and urged Ms. Edwards to check their registration. "We wouldn't have known had someone not come over here."

Lines at one Cobb County polling place Wednesday had ballooned into a three-hour wait for early voting. On a canvassing trip in Lilburn, Ga., targeting unlikely midterm voters, a group of domestic care workers who have been volunteering six days a week talked to multiple residents who worried about their registration status.

And on Monday, news that about 40 black seniors were barred from early voting at the behest of county officials in eastern Georgia's Jefferson County enraged voting rights advocates, who say such actions could have a chilling effect.

The group of seniors had planned to head to the polls on a decorated bus from the "Black Voters Matter Fund," a nonpartisan state group that encourages civic engagement among African-Americans. There was singing, joyous chants and a palpable sense of excitement until one of the directors of the group's living facility said a county worker had called and said the group could not board the bus and go vote.

The worker cited the appearance of partisanship, but the voting-rights group and its leaders were furious, saying the incident was a clear example of voter suppression.

"No racially discriminatory suppression of that right can be tolerated in Georgia or elsewhere," read a letter sent Wednesday by Leah Aden, an attorney at the NAACP Legal Defense Fund. "In this contested election season, we urge you all to protect against voter intimidation and other conduct designed to suppress voting rights in your County."

Cliff Albright, the co-founder of "Black Voters Matter," said the incident sparked memories of the Jim Crow South for some of the elderly voters they were attempting to bring to the polls.

"It seems incredible, but this is the daily realities in these counties," Mr. Albright said. "These are the connections and the circles of influence that a lot of people who don't live in these counties understand. They don't understand the levels of intimidation."

This fear — that state officials are intentionally attempting to undermine voting rights of minorities — echoes a darker period in America's past when states codified voter disenfranchisement along racial lines. The Georgia scenes have also reignited debate about the Supreme Court's 2013 ruling in Shelby County v. Holder, which eliminated the need for states with a history of voter disenfranchisement to obtain federal pre-clearance before changing its voting laws, as was previously required under a section of the Voting Rights Act of 1965.

"We've lost that pre-emptive mechanism, so now we're left with case-by-case litigation to fight, and that can be slow," said Kristen Clarke, the president of national Lawyers' Committee for Civil Rights Under Law. "We're in a moment that requires a tremendous amount of vigilance to be on top of the potential voter suppression efforts that are emanating around the country."

This is especially true in Georgia, which has long been watched by voting rights advocates. One prominent group, the Brennan Center for Justice at New York University, reported recently that the state had removed 1.5 million voters from its rolls between 2012 and 2016, twice the number of the preceding four years, and that elections also had seen a rise in provisional ballots that are submitted by voters whose registrations are somehow missing or defective. The group said that data suggests, but does not prove, that the customary process of purging voters who have moved or died from the rolls is also removing legitimate voters.

Mr. Kemp was a key proponent of the 2017 state law that requires an "exact match" between a voter's registration form and his or her government documents, meaning a missing hyphen, or a difference between a married and a maiden name, can cause a registration to be suspended.

Mr. Kemp resisted calls to resign from his post as secretary of state during his gubernatorial run. He has also repeatedly leveled the charge that Ms. Abrams wants noncitizens' votes to count, based on a recent campaign speech where Ms. Abrams said "the blue wave" should be "comprised of those who are documented and undocumented." Ms. Abrams has denied she meant that noncitizens should have their votes counted; she said she was referring to who Democrats are pledging to protect, if elected.

"I don't know what's worse: Actively working to undermine the rule of law by letting illegal immigrants vote or lying to hardworking Georgians about it," Mr. Kemp tweeted Wednesday. "Either way, Stacey Abrams is too extreme for Georgia."

Ms. Abrams' campaign has tried to use the debate to mobilize voters, but Greg Shufeldt, a professor at Butler University who studies elections, says the state has a serious and lasting problem surrounding confidence in the election system.

Georgia ranks 43rd out of 50 in election integrity, according to one of Mr. Shufeldt's measures, which grades things like state election administration and expert opinion surveys.

That ranking is emblematic of almost a decade of fights between election rights groups and Mr. Kemp. Questions have long swirled around Mr. Kemp's office about issues including voter data security and whether Georgia's voting machines were fit for modern elections.

A judge in September rejected one group's request to force Georgia to use paper ballots in the 2018 election. Still, in doing so, the judge wrote that "state election officials had buried their heads in the sand," about questions surrounding the state's election machinery.

A different lawsuit filed this week from election rights groups accused Mr. Kemp's office of "excessive rejection" of absentee ballots in Gwinnett County, which is electorally important, increasingly diverse, and beginning to lean liberal as the state's demographics change.

An analysis by the Atlanta Journal Constitution found that Gwinnett County had rejected about 8.5 percent of absentee ballots, while less than 2 percent had been rejected statewide.

"This is 2018 and I'm just not sure why this has to be this complicated," said Robert Thompson, who works in information technology and lives in Cobb County outside Atlanta. Mr. Thompson had to contact a voter hotline from the American Civil Liberties Union because his absentee ballot application kept being rejected. It ended up that his election office was using a spam blocker that prohibited his emails from being seen.

"People just give up because they don't have time for this," Mr. Thompson said.

Georgia is one of a few states that uses electronic-only voting machines without a paper trail to back up results. Election experts have frequently warned that such systems leave the state without recourse in the event of a severe election hacking or tampering.

Mr. Kemp nonetheless remains steadfast that Georgia has no voting rights issues. In 2016, he refused an offer by the Department of Homeland Security to help with election security, and called it an attempt to "subvert the Constitution to achieve the goal of federalizing elections under the guise of security."

He was one of few state election officials in America to reject federal assistance.

MICHAEL WINES contributed reporting from Washington.

Stacey Abrams Ends Fight for Georgia Governor With Harsh Words for Her Rival

BY ALAN BLINDER AND RICHARD FAUSSET | NOV. 16, 2018

ATLANTA — Stacey Abrams ended her Democratic bid to become governor of Georgia on Friday, acknowledging that she did not have the votes to beat her Republican rival, Brian Kemp, but sounding a defiant note by declaring that an "erosion of our democracy" had kept many of her backers from the polls.

The narrow defeat of Ms. Abrams, who would have become the first black woman to be elected governor anywhere in the United States, as well as the apparent loss of Andrew Gillum, who sought to become Florida's first black governor, at once illuminated the vestiges of Southern history and demonstrated how demographic changes have taken hold across the region and begun to reshape its politics.

The two candidates ran as unabashed liberals and their strong showings in two pivotal states where Democrats have lately struggled is likely to keep the debate going within the Democratic Party over the best strategy for making gains in 2020. There is significant internal disagreement over which candidates the party ought to put forward and how they should run.

The race between Ms. Abrams and Mr. Kemp pitted two versions of Georgia against one another. Ms. Abrams, 44, represented the diverse future of the state and its capital, Atlanta, home to black colleges and a hub of black political power. Mr. Kemp, 55, who bragged he had a pickup truck big enough to "round up criminal illegals," played to the state's rural voters and linked himself with President Trump. In the end, it was enough to allow the Republican Party to maintain its grip on power in Georgia, which has not elected a Democrat as governor since 1998.

Even before Ms. Abrams ended her campaign, Mr. Kemp had been preparing to take control. He declared victory two days after the election and appointed a chief of staff for his transition. He also resigned as secretary of state, ending his oversight of the election in which he was a candidate. When he appeared at the State Capitol last week, he asserted that he had won "a clear and convincing victory" and pledged to "put hard-working Georgians ahead of politics."

Ms. Abrams ran a type of campaign that modern Georgia had never seen before, relying on turnout among minority and low-frequency voters and championing an unflinchingly progressive message. In turn, she won in Democratic strongholds like Atlanta and Savannah, but also in the vote-rich Atlanta suburbs that were not long ago centers of Republican influence.

While every Southern state has its liberal-leaning cities surrounded by conservative countryside, the divide is particularly pronounced in Georgia because of metropolitan Atlanta's immensity, its central role in the American civil rights movement, and the rapidly growing number of nonwhite people who have been choosing to live in the city's sprawling suburbs, which were once destinations for white flight.

Rural Georgia certainly has swaths of racial moderation and iterations of conservatism that are detached from white grievance. But there are also political attitudes, and ways of expressing them, that stand in stark contrast to a capital that has long offered itself to the world as a beacon of racial comity.

Rural Georgia is a place where the Confederate flag, for complex reasons, is still embraced by many white residents as a proud symbol of heritage. And some still display it as an overt symbol of white supremacy.

"We're at least a pink state, if not a purple state," said Charles S. Bullock III, a professor of political science at the University of Georgia, of the close turnout. "Part of that is the demographic change that the Democrats have been counting on."

As recently as the late 1990s, Professor Bullock said, white Georgians cast roughly three-quarters of the state's votes. In 2016, that figure fell closer to 60 percent. And he said he would be unsurprised if the white share of the vote in this year's balloting turned out to be even lower.

Ms. Abrams, while acknowledging Friday that she could not win, did not concede either.

"More than 200 years into Georgia's democratic experiment, the state failed its voters," Ms. Abrams said, her voice alternating among anguish, contempt, frustration and outrage as she argued that "eight years of systemic disenfranchisement, disinvestment and incompetence had its desired effect on the electoral process in Georgia."

Still, it was the closest race for governor in Georgia since 1966. Ms. Abrams came within 18,000 votes of forcing a runoff, and about 55,000 votes of winning outright, in an election that drew almost four million ballots.

"Let's be clear: This is not a speech of concession because concession means to acknowledge an action is right, true or proper," Ms. Abrams said amid a blistering attack on Mr. Kemp's record as the state's chief elections regulator and on the balloting process in Georgia. "As a woman of conscience and faith, I cannot concede that."

As Ms. Abrams ended her campaign, she returned to a theme that had surfaced throughout: that Mr. Kemp, who was the Georgia secretary of state until the Thursday after the election, had used his position to suppress voting and ease his path into the governor's mansion.

Although she pledged to pray for Mr. Kemp, she also uncorked a bracing indictment of his tenure as secretary of state, including the election last week. She excoriated a system, overseen by Mr. Kemp and legions of local officials, that left voters lawfully purged from the rolls, waiting in the rain and facing rejections of their ballots for arbitrary reasons.

"Georgia citizens tried to exercise their constitutional rights and were still denied the ability to elect their leaders," she said. "Under

Brian Kemp, Georgia's former secretary of state, is positioned to maintain the Republican grip on power in Georgia, which has not elected a Democrat as governor since 1998.

the watch of the now former secretary of state, democracy failed Georgians of every political party, every race, every region. Again."

Mr. Kemp, who has defended his time as secretary of state and rebuffed Democratic attacks that he was an "architect of suppression," did not respond directly to Ms. Abrams's critiques on Friday night.

"The election is over and hardworking Georgians are ready to move forward," Mr. Kemp said in a statement. "We can no longer dwell on the divisive politics of the past but must focus on Georgia's bright and promising future."

The race presented residents with starkly different personalities, policies and visions for the nation's eighth-most populous state. In turn, the contest drew enormous attention and money, with more than $65 million in spending, including the primaries, and about 2.1 million early votes, easily breaking state records.

Mr. Kemp vowed to cut regulations and crack down on undocumented immigrants. He captured the Republican nomination in a July runoff, bolstered by Mr. Trump's support and by provocative television ads in which he brandished a shotgun at a teenager (to underscore his support for gun rights) and promised to round up "criminal illegals" in his pickup truck.

His proposals, though sometimes vague, thrilled conservatives: a "Track and Deport" plan that would "create a comprehensive database to track criminal aliens in Georgia;" new limits on the state's budget, sustaining the government's efforts to lure major economic projects; and an intensified focus on stopping gang activity.

He had not been the Republican establishment's first choice — the retiring Republican governor, Nathan Deal, endorsed one of Mr. Kemp's primary rivals before eventually offering his full-throated backing — and his hard-right tone sent waves of concern through the Georgia business community, which wields enormous influence.

Ms. Abrams, a Yale-educated tax lawyer raised by civil rights activists in coastal Mississippi, ran largely as an unapologetic liberal, promising to expand Medicaid under the Affordable Care Act as a way to address the state's acute rural health care problem.

Though she seemed most comfortable talking policy, her allies emphasized her place in the broader context of Southern history. In a campaign appearance, the television personality Oprah Winfrey spoke of the indignities suffered by nonwhite Georgians in the days of Jim Crow, saying that failing to vote now would be "disrespecting and disregarding" those ancestors.

And Democrats invested enormous hopes in Ms. Abrams's candidacy, betting that she would allow the party to rebound from a string of defeats in Georgia.

Each side in the race tried to paint the other as extremist. Mr. Trump called Ms. Abrams "one of the most extreme far-left politicians in the entire country" and said she would "have Georgia turn into Venezuela." Democrats said Mr. Kemp's shotgun ad showed him to be "reckless" and "irresponsible."

But the issue that seemed to electrify voters most in the final weeks was voting access, a particularly sensitive matter because Mr. Kemp was still overseeing elections.

Two days before the election, Mr. Kemp's office announced, citing scant evidence, that it was opening an inquiry into the state Democratic Party after what the office called "a failed attempt to hack the state's voter registration system." Democrats denied any wrongdoing and called the announcement a political stunt.

But Mr. Kemp's record still gave Ms. Abrams's campaign a rallying cry even after the polls closed: "Count every vote," her campaign manager repeatedly told the television cameras, asserting that it was not yet time for Ms. Abrams to concede.

On Friday evening in Atlanta, Ms. Abrams held true to that.

"I don't want to hold public office if I have to scheme my way into the post because the title of governor isn't nearly as important as our shared title — voters," she said. "And that is why we fight on."

Stacey Abrams: We Cannot Resign Ourselves to Dismay and Disenfranchisement

OPINION | BY STACEY ABRAMS | MAY 15, 2019

As more people of color claim political power, efforts to block them will accelerate — unless we act.

ATLANTA — In the mid-1960s, when my father was a teenager, he was arrested. His crime? Registering black voters in Mississippi. He and my mother had joined the civil rights movement well before they were even old enough to vote themselves.

They braved this dangerous work, which all too often created martyrs of marchers. In doing so, my parents ingrained in their six children a deep and permanent reverence for the franchise. We were taught that the right to vote undergirds all other rights, that free and fair elections are necessary for social progress.

That is why I am determined to end voter suppression and empower all people to participate in our democracy.

True voter access means that every person has the right to register, cast a ballot and have that ballot counted — without undue hardship. Unfortunately, the forces my parents battled 50 years ago continue to stifle democracy.

My home state, Georgia, for example, suffered a vicious blend of electoral malfeasance, misfeasance and mismanagement during my race for governor last fall. But Georgia is not alone.

Local and state officials across the country, emboldened by the Supreme Court effectively neutering the Voting Rights Act in Shelby County v. Holder in 2013, are shamelessly weakening voter registration, ballot access and ballot-counting procedures.

These officials slyly mask their assaults through criteria that appear neutral on the surface but nevertheless target race, gender, language and economic status. The "exact match" policy in Georgia, which a federal court deemed unlawful in November because it requires perfect data entry to secure a timely registration, serves as one example of such a policy.

Although "exact match" lacks the explicit racial animus of Jim Crow, its execution nonetheless betrayed its true purpose to disenfranchise voters of color. Georgia's secretary of state held 53,000 voter registrations hostage under exact match last year, 70 percent of which came from black voters, who made up only around 30 percent of Georgia's eligible voters.

The state officials behind exact match were well aware, per an earlier lawsuit, that when only a missing hyphen or a typo in a government database can form the basis to withhold the right to vote, people of color will bear the brunt of such trivial mistakes.

A particularly egregious example involved a voter whose last name is "del Rio." He was affected by the policy merely because the department of motor vehicles office where he registered to vote did not allow spaces in last names. He was "delRio" there. But the voter rolls do allow spaces. No exact match. Voters like Mr. del Rio faced unnecessary hurdles, and poll workers were not trained properly to make sure that voices like his were heard.

Across the country, voter purges employ an easily manipulated "use it or lose it" rule, under which eligible voters who exercised their First Amendment right to abstain from voting in prior elections can be booted off the rolls.

Add to this mix closed or relocated polling places outside the reach of public transit, sometimes as far as 75 miles away, or long lines that force low-income voters to forfeit half a day's pay, and a modern poll tax is revealed.

State legislatures have continued the trend this year. In Texas, officials are attempting to further criminalize eligible voters for inadvertent errors often caused by language barriers. In Tennessee, a state with notoriously low voter turnout, the legislature approved a bill subjecting third-party groups conducting voter registration drives to onerous requirements under threat of civil and criminal penalty.

In Florida, 1.4 million Floridians with felonies were re-enfranchised with a constitutional amendment last year that passed with 65 percent of the vote — the largest expansion of voting rights in a half-century. But the legislature has contravened the will of the people, once again disenfranchising hundreds of thousands of returning citizens through a bill that imposes an antiquated poll tax on them in the form of court fees.

After voters run gantlets to get on the rolls, they are undermined by the mismanagement of inexact voter databases, ancient and under-resourced machines, lost absentee ballots or by elections officials who refuse to count votes that were properly cast.

On election night 2018, as phones rang with tales of missing machines, provisional ballots allocated by a vague lottery system and regular voters vanishing from the rolls, I made a simple demand: Count every vote.

Over the next 10 days, my campaign logged over 40,000 calls of voter suppression, sent out volunteers to help voters make sure their provisional ballots were counted and quickly filed numerous lawsuits. Amid this chaos, the results of the election were certified. We demonstrated the immensity of the problem, yet opponents to voting rights responded with the specious claim that increased turnout was somehow proof that no suppression had occurred.

That argument is shameful. A record number of black, Latino and Asian-American/Pacific Islander voters turned out in Georgia to support an inclusive agenda, which led to even more of those voters being subjected to voter suppression.

Voters of color endured three-, four- and five-hour lines on Election Day precisely because so many who turned out to vote were confronted with under-resourced precincts and faulty voting machines. Unprecedented turnout led to countless thousands being blocked or turned away.

The state's top elections official, former Secretary of State Brian Kemp himself — functioning simultaneously as the scorekeeper, referee and contestant in the gubernatorial election — was caught revealing to supporters that he was "concerned" about record absentee ballot requests from voters of color.

In response, I redoubled my commitment to voting rights and started a nonprofit called Fair Fight Action to harness the commitment and urgency of Georgians who reported, by a 52 percent margin, that they believe suppression affected 2018 election outcomes.

This distrust, shared by millions of others nationwide, should alarm every American; democracy should not differ so dramatically across state and, worse, county lines, where hyperlocal suppressive tactics like the proposed closing of most polling places in a majority-black South Georgia county last year can slip under the radar.

That's why we filed a federal voting rights case three weeks after Election Day, demanding that Georgia's elections system comply with constitutional obligations and requirements under federal law, including those provisions of the Voting Rights Act that remain in force, and we asked that Georgia be required to pre-clear voting changes again with the Justice Department before taking effect.

We ask for proper and uniform training of poll workers, timely processing of absentee ballots, functioning and secure voting machines, accurate voter registration databases, an end to policies like "exact match" and "use it or lose it," and many more necessary remedies.

Facing an existential crisis of democracy, Americans cannot resign ourselves to disenfranchisement and dismay. We must find hope in the energy of voters who supported access to health care, economic opportunity and high-quality public education in record numbers.

This is our ethos: Use the ballot box to create the change our communities need and deserve. In Georgia and across our country, voters deserve the right to pick their leaders and set the direction of our nation. And we shall not rest until this democracy is fully realized.

STACEY ABRAMS is the founder of Fair Fight Action and was the Democratic nominee for governor in Georgia in 2018.

Stacey Abrams Will Not Run for President in 2020, Focusing Instead on Fighting Voter Suppression

BY ASTEAD W. HERNDON | AUG. 13, 2019

Ms. Abrams will concentrate on building a national movement for fair and equitable elections, including a voter protection hotline.

STACEY ABRAMS, the Georgia politician who captured national attention during her unsuccessful run for governor in 2018, has decided not to run for president after publicly contemplating a bid for months.

Ms. Abrams, a Democrat, will instead focus her efforts on preventing voter suppression with a new initiative called Fair Fight 2020, which takes its name from a group Ms. Abrams began last year after her election loss. It will work with state parties in battleground states to more closely monitor voter protection ahead of next year's general election.

Ms. Abrams announced her decision Tuesday afternoon at the International Union of Painters and Allied Trades convention in Las Vegas. Though she is sidestepping the crowded Democratic presidential field, she is likely to remain atop any Democratic nominee's vice-presidential wish list.

"There are only two things stopping us in 2020: that people have a reason to vote, and that they have the right to vote," Ms. Abrams said. "I've decided to leave it to a whole bunch of other people to make sure they have a reason to vote."

The decision by Ms. Abrams, a former Democratic leader in the Georgia House of Representatives, ends months of speculation, some of which was fueled by Ms. Abrams herself. Repeatedly, she has said she believes she is qualified to be in the presidential field, and she has held several private meetings with other candidates, encouraging them to focus on voter suppression and fair elections as they crisscross the country for votes.

"My job is to be the voice to those who do not believe they are heard," she said Tuesday, asking the crowd to chant, "Fair fight! Fair fight! Fair fight!"

In last year's election for governor, Ms. Abrams narrowly lost to Brian Kemp, a Republican who was Georgia's secretary of state and in charge of the state's voter rolls. Civil rights groups raised questions about voter suppression and election rigging in Georgia throughout the race, including when Mr. Kemp's office closed several polling stations in predominantly black areas and stalled more than 50,000 voter applications in the run-up to the election.

Ms. Abrams made her decision in recent days, aides said, as she determined she was comfortable with the current crop of Democratic candidates.

Previously, Ms. Abrams turned down a pitch from Senator Chuck Schumer, the minority leader, to run for Senate in Georgia.

"In typical Stacey Abrams fashion, she's taken a hard look on the best use of her time and talents are," said Lauren Groh-Wargo, a close aide to Ms. Abrams and her campaign manager in 2018. "And while being a pundit or running for president might have been easier, fighting voter suppression and making sure our nominees have what they need to fight on the ground is what's most important."

Beto O'Rourke, the Texas Democrat who launched a presidential bid after a failed 2018 Senate run, commented on Ms. Abrams's decision to stay out the race.

"We can't solve any of the challenges we face — from health care to gun violence to climate change — without fixing our democracy," Mr. O'Rourke tweeted. "Thank you, @StaceyAbrams, for your leadership."

Earlier this year, Ms. Abrams delivered the Democratic response to President Trump's State of the Union speech, earning rave reviews from party leaders. In it, she blended lofty rhetoric with pragmatic policy proposals, a combination that some of her supporters argue is ideal for a Democratic candidate hoping to defeat Mr. Trump.

Others have touted her good standing with black voters across the ideological spectrum, which could increase turnout among a critical constituency that was less than enthused about the 2016 Democratic ticket. In the last presidential election, black voter turnout dropped for the first time in two decades, according to Pew Research statistics.

Ms. Abrams was sure to face challenges had she entered the already-sprawling Democratic presidential field, where several candidates with higher national name recognition have already struggled to break through. She would have had to quickly build out a national fund-raising operation, and face off against several allies who acted as surrogates and fund-raisers for Ms. Abrams during her campaign for governor.

She would also have to face the same restrictive voting laws that, according to Ms. Abrams, stymied her in 2018.

"I can't undo the election in 2018 and didn't even try," Ms. Abrams said Tuesday in Las Vegas, "but I will say something that seems to anger people when I say it: We won. We won that election."

It has now become commonplace for Democratic presidential candidates to echo Ms. Abrams's refrain on the campaign trail and say that they believe she would have defeated Mr. Kemp had the election been free of suppression allegations.

"Massive voter suppression prevented Stacey Abrams from becoming the rightful governor of Georgia," Senator Elizabeth Warren of Massachusetts said in an April speech.

In November, shortly after the election, Senator Cory Booker of New Jersey said, "I think that Stacey Abrams's election is being stolen from her, using what I think are insidious measures to disenfranchise certain groups of people."

Since her loss to Mr. Kemp, Ms. Abrams has thrust her star power behind Fair Fight Action, the advocacy group she began to "expand democracy and ensure all voters have access to the polls."

The group's latest initiative will expand beyond Georgia to target

20 states, including across the Midwest and Southeast, and will invest up to $5 million.

It will work to correct inaccurate voter rolls, address shortages of voting machines and provisional ballots, and standardize the rules around counting absentee ballots, according to aides. There will also be a state-by-state hotline where election irregularities can be reported.

Fair Fight Action is currently suing the Georgia secretary of state's office, asking federal courts to address voting procedures that the group claims are unconstitutional and discriminatory.

ASTEAD W. HERNDON is a national political reporter based in New York. He was previously a Washington-based political reporter and a City Hall reporter for The Boston Globe.

Stacey Abrams Is Playing the Long Game for Our Democracy

OPINION | BY MELANYE PRICE | AUG. 15, 2019

And she's playing to win.

EVERYWHERE SHE GOES, Stacey Abrams is treated like a rock star — or a presidential candidate. I and all my friends wanted her to jump into the presidential race. Instead, she's doing something more important. She's creating an apparatus to fight voter suppression across the country, a prize that's essential to a fair and functioning democracy.

"No matter which ones of our nominees win, if we haven't fought this scourge," she told a reporter, "if we haven't pushed back against Moscow Mitch and his determination to block any legislation that would cure our voting machines, then we are all in a world of trouble." (She remains open to being a vice-presidential pick down the line.)

For at least the next 15 months, her organization will train staff members in 20 competitive and battleground states to help fix inaccurate voter rolls, address shortages of voting machines and provisional ballots and formalize the rules around counting absentee ballots. They will also work to increase participation in the 2020 census.

This will have even more of an impact than a presidential run. Her work on voter suppression could reshape the electoral landscape so it resembles the years after Voting Rights Act of 1965, when new constituencies were created and a new political leadership class emerged. Her work could help get more Democrats elected at the local and state levels and grease the pipeline to the presidency for future generations. That's also true for governors and senators.

Ms. Abrams is also seeking to empower citizens at the local levels of government. Seemingly small decisions — which cases will be tried, which schools will be shut down, how many seats are on the water board — often have an enormous impact on the lives of people of color.

Stronger voter protections for those hyper-local races could make a big difference.

The unique skills and experiences she acquired while running her campaign set her up for success. She flipped the formula on how politicians usually run for office. She trusted the expertise and networks of women of color who are civic engagement organizers, pouring resources into their efforts early on. She expanded the electorate. She talked about race and identity on the stump. She traversed the state, speaking to white people in counties that hadn't voted for a Democrat since Lyndon B. Johnson. She explained to them why her diverse coalition would also benefit them, whether or not they chose to vote for her.

As a result, more white Democrats in Georgia voted for her than any for any candidate since Bill Clinton. Her campaign doubled youth turnout; tripled Latino turnout; and tripled Asian-Pacific Islander turnout. In 2014, 1.1 million Georgians voted on the Democratic side. But four years later, 1.2 million African-Americans voted for her.

But the thing that kept Ms. Abrams from the governorship is the thing that is keeping other African-Americans and people of color from office in many places — voter suppression. "My mission is to make certain that no one has to go through in 2020 what we went through in 2018," she said in a speech this week.

Her opponent, Brian Kemp, had created such an obstacle course of discrimination, no one can really say that the election was fair. As secretary of state during the campaign, he held 53,000 voter registrations hostage under the exact match law, which penalized typos, missing hyphens and other tiny things. Seven out of 10 of those registrations came from black voters, who made up only around 30 percent of eligible voters. He purged rolls, reduced the number of polling machines and did many other things to limit the impact of black voters in the state. Incidentally, he molded the electoral landscape to favor him. Sadly, Ms. Abrams also has experience going toe-to-toe with politicians who are determined to block minorities from the ballot box.

Stacey Abrams speaking at a DNC gala in June.

Ms. Abrams's focus on the state and local levels is crucial because the 2013 decision in Shelby County v. Holder weakened the federal government's ability to protect people of color from voter suppression. Without the federal safety net of preclearance, many states are free to enact discriminatory voter restrictions and find new ways to diminish and dilute minority votes. That leaves teams of lawyers, organizers, citizens and elected officials to fight voter suppression state-by-state. But if African-Americans and other minority voters are to place their confidence in anyone's ability to facilitate this movement, it would be Stacey Abrams.

While Barack Obama's presidency remains a high point in African-American politics, his success arguably catalyzed a renewed effort among people who want to make sure he will be the only black president for the foreseeable future and that other minority groups will never get a chance.

In the wake of his 2008 victory, Republican state officials immediately enacted burdensome and unnecessary voting restrictions. And in 2018 we saw the full effects of the Supreme Court's devastating decision in Shelby County v. Holder. Voter suppression played a key role in narrow Democratic losses by Ms. Abrams, Andrew Gillum and Beto O'Rourke — three Deep South states that could be in play for Democrats with a fair voting process.

That's why Ms. Abrams's new movement is vital. The work of building and strengthening our democracy is often done by independent third-party groups, run by women of color, who are expert at long-term organizing, canvassing and turnout, like the New Florida Majority and the New Virginia Majority. Their work benefits every citizen, regardless of political affiliation. Ms. Abrams and others are laying the foundation for a more diverse and equitable electorate and political leadership. She deserves all of our support.

MELANYE PRICE, a professor of political science at Prairie View A&M University in Texas, is the author, most recently, of "The Race Whisperer: Barack Obama and the Political Uses of Race."

CHAPTER 5

The Future of Voting

In the run-up to the 2020 presidential election, the partisan divide on voting rights continued. House Democrats, after taking the majority in January 2019, made the expansion of voting rights their top priority, passing a bill that would combat various forms of voter suppression; it was blocked in the Republican-led Senate and did not become law. In 2016, Russian disinformation operations sought to explicitly and implicitly discourage black voters from going to the polls, and many observers feared that Russian interference would continue to threaten the integrity of American elections.

Vote. That's Just What They Don't Want You to Do.

EDITORIAL | **BY THE NEW YORK TIMES** | **MARCH 10, 2018**

The editorial board represents the opinions of the board, its editor and the publisher. It is separate from the newsroom and the Op-Ed section.

THIS IS A fragile moment for the nation. The integrity of democratic institutions is under assault from without and within, and basic standards of honesty and decency in public life are corroding. If you are horrified at what is happening in Washington and in many states, you can march in the streets, you can go to town halls and demand more from your representatives, you can share the latest outrageous news on your social media feed — all worthwhile activities. But none of it matters if you don't go out and vote.

It's a perennial conundrum for the world's oldest democracy: Why do so many Americans fail to go to the polls? Some abstainers think that they're registering a protest against the awful choices. They're fooling themselves. Nonvoters aren't protesting anything; they're just putting their lives and futures in the hands of the people who probably don't want them to vote. We've seen recently what can happen when people choose instead to take their protest to the ballot box. We saw it in Virginia in November. We saw it, to our astonishment, in Alabama in December. We may see it this week in western Pennsylvania. Voting matters.

Casting a ballot is the best opportunity most of us will ever get to have a say in who will represent us, what issues they will address and how they will spend our money. The right to vote is so basic, President Lyndon Johnson said in 1965, that without it "all others are meaningless."

And yet every election, tens of millions of Americans stay home. Studies of turnout among developed nations consistently rank the United States near the bottom. In the most recent midterms, in 2014, less than 37 percent of eligible voters went to the polls — the lowest turnout in more than 70 years. In 2016, 102 million people didn't vote, far more than voted for any single candidate.

The problem isn't just apathy, of course. Keeping people from voting has been an American tradition from the nation's earliest days, when the franchise was restricted to white male landowners. It took a civil war, constitutional amendments, violently suppressed activism against discrimination and a federal act enforcing the guarantees of those amendments to extend this basic right to every adult. With each expansion of voting rights, the nation inched closer to being a truly representative democracy. Today, only one group of Americans may be legally barred from voting — those with felony records, a cruel and pointless restriction that disproportionately silences people of color.

In the months leading up to the midterm elections on Nov. 6, when the House, Senate and statehouses around the country are up for grabs, the editorial board will explore the complicated question of why

Americans don't vote, and what can be done to overcome the problem. The explanations fall into three broad categories.

SUPPRESSION A 96-year-old woman in Tennessee was denied a voter-ID card despite presenting four forms of identification, including her birth certificate. A World War II veteran was turned away in Ohio because his Department of Veterans Affairs photo ID didn't include his address. Andrea Anthony, a 37-year-old black woman from Wisconsin who had voted in every major election since she was 18, couldn't vote in 2016 because she had lost her driver's license a few days before.

Stories like these are distressingly familiar, as more and more states pass laws that make voting harder for certain groups of voters, usually minorities, but also poor people, students and the elderly. They require forms of photo identification that minorities are much less likely to have or be able to get — purportedly to reduce fraud, of which there is virtually no evidence. They eliminate same-day registration, close polling stations in minority areas and cut back early-voting hours and Sunday voting.

These new laws may not be as explicitly discriminatory as the poll taxes or literacy tests of the 20th century, but they are part of the same long-term project to keep minorities from the ballot box. And because African-Americans vote overwhelmingly for Democrats, the laws are nearly always passed by Republican-dominated legislatures.

In a lawsuit challenging Wisconsin's strict new voter-ID law, a former staff member for a Republican lawmaker testified that Republicans were "politically frothing at the mouth" at the prospect that the law would drive down Democratic turnout. It worked: After the 2016 election, one survey found that the law prevented possibly more than 17,000 registered voters, disproportionately poor and minority, from voting. Donald Trump carried the state by fewer than 23,000 votes.

FAILING TECHNOLOGY The legitimacy of an election is only as good as the reliability of the machines that count the votes. And yet 43 states use voting machines that are no longer being made, and are at or near the end of their useful life. Many states still manage their voter-registration rolls using software programs from the 1990s. It's no surprise that this sort of infrastructure failure hits poorer and minority areas harder, often creating hourslong lines at the polls and discouraging many voters from coming out at all. Upgrading these machines nationwide would cost at least $1 billion, maybe much more, and Congress has consistently failed to provide anything close to sufficient funding to speed along the process.

Elections are hard to run with aging voting technology, but at least those problems aren't intentional. Hacking and other types of interference are. In 2016, Russian hackers were able to breach voter registration systems in Illinois and several other states, and targeted dozens more. They are interfering again in advance of the 2018 midterms, according to intelligence officials, who are demanding better cyber-security measures. These include conducting regular threat assessments, using voting machines that create paper trails and conducting postelection audits. Yet President Trump, who sees any invocation of Russian interference as a challenge to the legitimacy of his election, consistently downplays or dismisses these threats. Meanwhile, Mr. Trump's State Department has not spent a dime of the $120 million Congress allocated to it to fight disinformation campaigns by Russia and other countries.

DISILLUSIONMENT Some people wouldn't vote if you put a ballot box in their living room. Whether they believe there is no meaningful difference between the major parties or that the government doesn't care what they think regardless of who is in power, they have detached themselves from the political process.

That attitude is encouraged by many in government, up to and including the current president, who cynically foster feelings of disillusionment by hawking fake tales of rigged systems and illegal voters, even as they raise millions of dollars from wealthy donors and draw legislative maps to entrench their power.

The disillusionment is understandable, and to some degree it's justified. But it creates a self-fulfilling prophecy. When large numbers of people don't vote, elections are indeed decided by narrow, unrepresentative groups and in the interests of wealth and power. The public can then say, See? We were right. They don't care about us. But when more people vote, the winning candidates are more broadly representative and that improves government responsiveness to the public and enhances democratic legitimacy.

These obstacles to voting and political participation are very real, and we don't discount their impact on turnout. The good news is there are fixes for all of them.

The most important and straightforward fix is to make it easier for people to register and vote. Automatic voter registration, which first passed in Oregon just three years ago, is now the law or practice in nine states, both red and blue, and the District of Columbia. Washington State is on the cusp of becoming the tenth, and New Jersey and Nevada may be close behind. More people also turn out when states increase voting opportunities, such as by providing mail-in ballots or by expanding voting hours and days.

The courts should be a bulwark protecting voting rights, and many lower federal courts have been just that in recent years, blocking the most egregious attacks on voting in states from North Carolina to Wisconsin. But the Supreme Court under Chief Justice John Roberts Jr. has made this task much harder, mainly by gutting a key provision of the Voting Rights Act in a 2013 case. Decisions like that one, which split 5 to 4, depend heavily on who is sitting in those nine seats — yet another reason people should care who gets elected.

In the end, the biggest obstacle to more Americans voting is their own sense of powerlessness. It's true: Voting is a profound act of faith, a belief that even if your voice can't change policy on its own, it makes a difference. Consider the attitude of Andrea Anthony, the Wisconsin woman who was deterred by the state's harsh new voter-ID law after voting her whole adult life. "Voting is important to me because I know I have a little, teeny, tiny voice, but that is a way for it to be heard," Ms. Anthony said. "Even though it's one vote, I feel it needs to count."

She's right. The future of America is in your hands. More people voting would not only mean "different political parties with different platforms and different candidates," the writer Rebecca Solnit said. "It would change the story. It would change who gets to tell the story."

There are a lot of stories desperately needing to be told right now, but they won't be as long as millions of Americans continue to sit out elections. Lament the state of the nation as much as you want. Then get out and vote.

A New Class of Voting Rights Activists Picks Up the Mantle in Mississippi

BY AUDRA D. S. BURCH | SEPT. 25, 2018

OXFORD, MISS. — The first time Howard Kirschenbaum registered voters in Mississippi was during the summer of 1964, when he was arrested and thrown in jail. The second time was on Tuesday, after returning to the Southern state more than a half-century later to support a new generation of voting rights activists.

In the quiet of a rainy morning, Mr. Kirschenbaum helped to register students on the campus of the University of Mississippi, and before long, he was in tears. Memories of Freedom Summer 1964, the historic campaign to register African-American voters in Mississippi, came rushing back.

"In that moment, there must have been five or six students, all waiting patiently to fill out the registration form," said Mr. Kirschenbaum, 73, recalling the summer he spent in Moss Point, Miss., 54 years ago. "I am witnessing this moment. They want to vote. They are able to vote. The connection between then and now was so palpable. This is what we worked for all those years ago."

Four veteran volunteers of Freedom Summer, now in their 70s and mostly retired, returned to the state this week to join a nonpartisan youth group, Mississippi Votes, for a voter registration campaign called Up2Us. Young and old, two full generations apart, gathered at a Jackson church, in nearby neighborhoods, on the balcony of an Oxford bookstore to talk about the perils and stakes of voter activism, then and now.

More than 50 years after Freedom Summer, with voting rights across the nation being whittled away by stricter requirements — requirements challenged in two Mississippi lawsuits as discriminatory — a new generation of youth are taking up the cause to increase voter registration and civic engagement, especially among young citizens and marginalized communities.

Howard Kirschenbaum, right, helped students at the University of Mississippi register to vote on Tuesday. Mr. Kirschenbaum is a veteran volunteer of the Freedom Summer 1964.

"There is a power that transcends our ages," said Arekia Bennett, 25, executive director of Mississippi Votes, which has 250 volunteers and chapters on nine different college campuses across the state. "We want to dive deep into the veteran stories and learn the lessons of that summer so we can shift the narrative, make our own changes in Mississippi."

With midterm elections less than two months away and two Senate seats up for grabs, Mississippi Votes is canvassing the state, as the volunteers before them did, hoping to chip away at the hundreds of thousands of unregistered voters. In total, there are about 1,839,449 registered voters in Mississippi, according to the secretary of state. Since August, Mississippi Votes has registered about 2,000.

"This is about creating a culture of civic engagement, not just during the election season. We want people to understand the political landscape and be involved on and off the clock," said Ms. Bennett, a

Arekia Bennett, center, the executive director of Mississippi Votes, at her office in Jackson, Miss.

Jackson State University graduate who wanted to be a physics teacher before turning to civic activism. "We want to engage and empower people so that they see themselves not just as a number but as a viable character in their own lives. This is about self-determination."

SIMILAR CHALLENGES, BUT CHANGING METHODS

In 1964, more than 700 college students — mostly white, mostly from the North — brought national attention and public fury to a state that audaciously, violently resisted change. They spent 10 weeks that summer registering voters. Their actions helped shape the framework of the civil rights movement and led, in part, to the 1965 Voting Rights Act.

In Mississippi cities and towns, they worked with local black activists, already steeped in the fight, to dismantle the laws and practices that made it almost impossible for African-Americans to vote. Barriers came in the form of poll taxes and literacy tests, along with the looming threat of persecution and violence. Led by the Council of Federated Organizations, a coalition of civil rights groups, the registration drive was as much about social equality and racism as it was about the power of each vote, the most fundamental tool in the democratic process.

The Voting Rights Act prohibited racial discrimination at the ballot box. But in 2013, the Supreme Court sharply reduced a key provision that required select states with a history of discrimination to seek federal approval before making changes in voting rules that could affect minorities.

Some states have also enacted rigorous guidelines that voting-rights advocates say amount to voter suppression. Some polling places have been eliminated, early voting opportunities have been cut back and voters in some states are now required to present photo identification. Before 2006, no state required a photo ID to vote.

In Mississippi, two recent lawsuits filed by the Southern Poverty Law Center and the Mississippi Center for Justice target the state's collection of so-called disenfranchising crimes. Offenses ranging from nonviolent charges, such as bribery and forgery, to carjacking and murder are used to disqualify voters. Critics argue that this system, said to be rooted in an 1890 law designed to curb black voters, disproportionately affects African-Americans.

A Mississippi Today study showed that about 56,000 Mississippians were banned from voting because of felony charges over a 23-year period starting in 1994. African-Americans represent 36 percent of Mississippi's total voting-age population, but make up about 61 percent of those who are ineligible to vote.

"The methods have become more sophisticated, but the broader issues are still in play," said Jim Kates, one of the Freedom veterans who, along with others, returned to Mississippi to assist Ms. Bennett and the other young organizers.

A LESSON OF FEAR AND HOPE

Part of what made Freedom Summer, first called the Mississippi Summer Project, so successful was that it exposed the horrors blacks faced trying to assert basic citizenship. Those experiences were exported to the masses in stark news dispatches. The volunteers, recruited by the Student Non-Violent Coordinating Committee and Congress of Racial Equality activists, trained at an Ohio college, then traveled some 800 miles south by bus or car.

At great personal risk, hundreds of black families hosted the volunteers in their homes. In turn, the volunteers met at black churches, to distribute registration information, helped to fill out forms and escorted them to the courthouses.

The veterans remembered a summer wrapped in fear but also hope. The volunteers were harassed by both the police and white residents. They were arrested and jailed. Beaten. Firebombed. And they were murdered. In the first week of the project, three activists — Andrew Goodman, Michael Schwerner and James Chaney — were abducted and shot just outside Philadelphia, Miss. Their corpses, brutalized and buried, were discovered two months later.

"You never really felt safe. And you never knew if some kind of harassment was going to turn into something more," said Benjamin Graham, 73, who left the University of California, Berkeley, to spend that summer in Mississippi.

Mr. Graham, who later became a doctor specializing in internal medicine, still remembers with chilling clarity lying in bed one summer night in the house of a Batesville family. It was his first night back in Mississippi after a quick return trip to California. Suddenly, around 2 a.m. his chest began to tighten. His breath had shortened and he was wheezing.

"I started feeling really bad and I honestly believed I had been poisoned by the KKK," said Mr. Graham, then 19. "It turns out I had asthma, but that just gives you a sense of the kind of stress we were under."

BUILDING TRUST IN DIFFERENT COMMUNITIES

On Saturday, after an afternoon of training at a church, then canvassing in Jackson neighborhoods, the group — veterans and students from

Jackson State University and Tougaloo College — locked arms, forming an intergenerational circle. Then they sang "We Shall Overcome."

The veterans later drove about 160 miles north to Oxford. They met with more Mississippi Vote student volunteers, from the University of Mississippi, and dined at a soul food diner on the town square. There they chatted about the joy of Southern cuisine and the dearth of rural hospitals and identity politics, but always, always returned to the summer of 1964.

John Strand talked about knocking on doors and trying to convince African-Americans to come to local churches for evening meetings where they could learn more about voter registration. Mr. Graham shared what he believed was one of their biggest responsibilities: bringing a certain understanding and sensitivity into the homes of black voters.

"We were asking people to do something big. There were huge risks for blacks to register to vote at the time. One way they were intimidated was by the practice of putting their names in the local newspaper if they registered to vote," he said. "That could cost them their jobs. Or more."

Mr. Graham paused and his words seemed to hang in the air. John Chappell, 21, one of the student Mississippi Vote organizers, turned to Graham and asked: How did you get people to trust you?

"You had to be willing to listen. I think they trusted us, but they didn't trust that things were going to be okay. And we didn't say they would," Graham said. "We knew the risks and we had to be honest about that."

How Voter Suppression
Could Swing the Midterms

OPINION | BY ARI BERMAN | OCT. 27, 2018

Campaigns are in the final dash to make sure people show up at the polls. But that doesn't matter if you're being systematically disenfranchised.

IN THE WEEKS before an election, political campaigns are focused on getting voters to the polls — holding rallies, knocking on doors and making phone calls to make sure people show up.

In Georgia and other states, the question in this election is not just about which candidates voters will support, but whether they'll be able to cast a ballot in the first place. The fight over voting rights in the midterms is a reminder that elections are not solely about who is running, what their commercials say or how many people are registered to vote. They are about who is allowed to vote and which officials are placing obstacles in the way of would-be voters.

The issue of voter suppression has exploded in recent weeks, most notably in the Georgia governor's race between Stacey Abrams, a Democrat, and Brian Kemp, a Republican. While running for higher office, Mr. Kemp, as secretary of state, also enforces Georgia's voting laws. This month, The Associated Press reported that Mr. Kemp's office had put more than 53,000 voter registration applications in limbo because the information on the forms did not exactly match state databases. Seventy percent of the pending registrations were from African-Americans, leading Ms. Abrams to charge that Mr. Kemp was trying "to tilt the playing field in his favor." Mr. Kemp claimed a voter registration group tied to Ms. Abrams had "submitted sloppy forms."

Since the 2010 election, 24 states overwhelmingly controlled by Republicans have put in place new voting restrictions, such as tougher voter ID laws, cutbacks to early voting and barriers to registration. Republicans say these measures are necessary to combat the threat of widespread voter fraud, even though study after study shows that such fraud is exceedingly rare. Many of these states have hotly contested races in 2018, and a drop in turnout among Democratic constituencies, such as young people and voters of color, could keep Republicans in power.

This month, the Supreme Court upheld a law in North Dakota that could block 70,000 residents who don't have a qualifying ID from the polls, including 5,000 Native American voters. The law is particularly burdensome for Native Americans because it requires an ID with a "current residential street address," but some Native Americans live on reservations and get their mail through post-office boxes. This is worrisome news for Senator Heidi Heitkamp, a Democrat, who is trailing her Republican opponent in the polls. She won election to the Senate in 2012 by 3,000 votes, thanks largely to 80 percent support from the two counties with large Indian reservations.

In Florida, where Andrew Gillum, a Democrat, is running for governor — he would be the state's first black governor — 1.6 million ex-felons won't be able to vote in this year's election, including almost half a million African-Americans. Florida is one of only four states that prevent ex-felons from voting unless they're pardoned by the governor. The architect of the current law, Gov. Rick Scott, a Republican, is running for the Senate. Mr. Scott's predecessor, Gov. Charlie Crist, a Republican who later switched parties, restored voting rights to 155,000 ex-felons; of those who registered to vote in 2012, 59 percent signed up as Democrats.

But Mr. Scott, who won two elections as governor by just 60,000 votes, reversed that policy and has restored voting rights to just a little more than 3,000 people while in office, with white ex-felons twice as likely to have their rights restored compared with African-Americans. He's now locked in a dead heat with Senator Bill Nelson, a Democrat. Though there's an amendment on the ballot that would restore voting rights to up to 1.4 million ex-felons in the state, those directly impacted by Mr. Scott's felon disenfranchisement law won't be able to vote

Could Blocking Voters Swing Elections?

A comparison of winning vote margins in recent elections and voter restrictions or purges in those same states.

MARGINS OF VICTORY VS. DISENFRANCHISED VOTERS

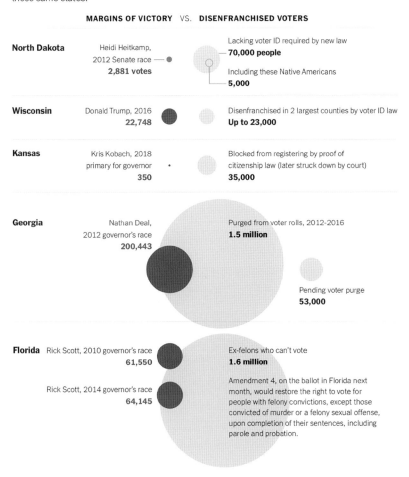

North Dakota

Heidi Heitkamp, 2012 Senate race — ● 2,881 votes

Lacking voter ID required by new law
70,000 people

Including these Native Americans
5,000

Wisconsin

Donald Trump, 2016
22,748

Disenfranchised in 2 largest counties by voter ID law
Up to 23,000

Kansas

Kris Kobach, 2018 primary for governor
350

Blocked from registering by proof of citizenship law (later struck down by court)
35,000

Georgia

Nathan Deal, 2012 governor's race
200,443

Purged from voter rolls, 2012-2016
1.5 million

Pending voter purge
53,000

Florida

Rick Scott, 2010 governor's race
61,550

Rick Scott, 2014 governor's race
64,145

Ex-felons who can't vote
1.6 million

Amendment 4, on the ballot in Florida next month, would restore the right to vote for people with felony convictions, except those convicted of murder or a felony sexual offense, upon completion of their sentences, including parole and probation.

BILL MARSH/THE NEW YORK TIMES

this year. Nearly 100,000 people who were on track to get their rights restored under Mr. Crist lost that chance when Mr. Scott changed the rules — a stark example of the precariousness of voting rights.

Voter suppression isn't just a potential problem in 2018 — it seems to have already had a decisive impact in recent years. In 2016, the year of the first presidential election with Wisconsin's voter ID law in place, the state saw a plunge in black voter turnout, which undoubtedly helped Donald Trump carry the state. A study by the University of Wisconsin-Madison found that the ID requirement kept up to 23,000 people from voting in two of the state's most Democratic counties, Milwaukee County and Madison's Dane County; African-Americans were more than three times as likely as whites to be deterred from voting by the law. Mr. Trump won the state by 23,000 votes. "It is very probable," Milwaukee's top election official, Neil Albrecht, told me last year, that "enough people were prevented from voting to have changed the outcome of the presidential election in Wisconsin." The ID requirement remains in effect today, and its biggest cheerleader, the Republican governor, Scott Walker, who claimed it was "a load of crap" that the law kept people from the polls, is locked in a close race for re-election against Tony Evers, a Democrat.

The most vociferous supporter of tightening access to the ballot, the Kansas Secretary of State, Kris Kobach, former vice chairman of President Trump's election integrity commission, is also running for governor this year. A voter ID law Mr. Kobach championed led to a 2 percent decrease in turnout in 2012, according to a study by the Government Accountability Office, with the largest drop-off among young, black and newly registered voters. Mr. Kobach won his primary in the governor's race by just 350 votes and is now in an extremely tight race against Laura Kelly, a Democrat, and an independent candidate, Greg Orman, so even a tiny reduction in participation among Democratic constituencies could put him in the governor's mansion. Since Mr. Kobach became secretary of state in 2011, more than 1,200 ballots have been tossed because voters showed up at the polls without a sufficient ID, a much larger number than the 15 cases of voter fraud his office has prosecuted.

Nowhere have hopes for high Democratic turnout collided with the reality of suppressive voting laws more than in Texas. In 2016, there were three million unregistered voters of color in the state, including

2.2 million unregistered Latinos and 750,000 unregistered African-Americans. Though Texas set a new voter registration record this year, it's unlikely that the number of unregistered Latinos and African-Americans has changed much. Texas has the most restrictive voter registration law in the country — to register voters, you must be deputized by a county and can register voters only in the county you're deputized in. The number of unregistered voters of color is a major obstacle for the Democratic candidate Beto O'Rourke in his race against Senator Ted Cruz. Though the demographics of the state suggest that it should be trending purple, the state's voting rules help keep it red.

Chief Justice John Roberts, in the 2013 Supreme Court ruling he wrote that gutted the Voting Rights Act, dismissed the idea that voting discrimination was still "flagrant" and "widespread." Instead he wrote, "Our country has changed." Yet since that decision, state and local governments that formerly had to approve their voting changes with the federal government, like Georgia and Texas, have closed 20 percent more polling places per capita than other states have, many in neighborhoods with large minority populations. More than half the states freed from federal oversight have put in place new voting restrictions in recent years. The 2016 election had the unfortunate distinction of being the first presidential contest in 50 years without the full protections of the Voting Rights Act; in 2018, the threat of disenfranchisement has gotten worse, in the South and beyond.

People tend to focus on obstacles to voting when they believe it will affect a close election, as in Georgia. But efforts to erect barriers to the ballot box are wrong regardless of whether they decide the outcome of an election. If Democrats turn out in large numbers on Nov. 6, as the early-voting data suggests is happening in some key states, it will be in spite of these barriers, not because they didn't exist or didn't matter.

Despite rampant suppression efforts, there is some hope. In seven states, ballot initiatives would restore voting rights to ex-felons, make it easier to register to vote and crack down on gerrymandering. If these pass, we could see 2018 as a turning point for expanding voting rights, instead of an election tainted by voter suppression. But first people need to have the right to cast a ballot.

ARI BERMAN, a senior reporter for Mother Jones, is the author of "Give Us the Ballot: The Modern Struggle for Voting Rights in America."

'They Don't Really Want Us to Vote': How Republicans Made It Harder

BY DANNY HAKIM AND MICHAEL WINES | NOV. 3, 2018

PRAIRIE VIEW, TEX. — Damon Johnson is a 19-year-old sophomore studying chemical engineering at historically black Prairie View A&M University. He's learning a lot about voting, too.

Mr. Johnson is one of the plaintiffs in a lawsuit filed last month by the NAACP Legal Defense and Educational Fund alleging that rural Waller County has tried to disenfranchise students at the university over decades, most recently by curtailing early voting on campus.

The polling station at the university's student center was restricted to three days of early voting, compared with two weeks in some other parts of the county — and two weeks at majority-white Texas A&M in a nearby county.

"I don't want this to be the reason, but it looks like we're PVAMU in a predominantly white area and they don't really want us to vote," Mr. Johnson said recently.

Limiting access to voting is rooted deep in American history, beginning with the founding fathers and peaking during the Jim Crow era in the South. But in the wake of the civil rights movement and the Voting Rights Act of 1965, the idea that disenfranchising legitimate voters was unethical, and even un-American, gained traction.

No more. Almost two decades after the Bush v. Gore stalemate led to voting rules being viewed as key elements of election strategy, the issue is playing an extraordinary role in the midterm elections.

Restrictions on voting, virtually all imposed by Republicans, reflect rising partisanship, societal shifts producing a more diverse America, and the weakening of the Voting Rights Act by the Supreme Court in 2013.

In North Dakota, Republicans passed an ID law that disproportionally affected Native Americans, strong supporters of the state's

Damon Johnson, a sophomore at Prairie View A&M University in Texas, voted on campus on Tuesday.

Democratic senator, Heidi Heitkamp, who is in an uphill fight. In Florida, New Hampshire, Texas and Wisconsin, among others, out-of-state university students face unusual hurdles to casting ballots.

On the Turtle Mountain Reservation in North Dakota, Native American voters are scrambling to comply with a restrictive voter ID law in time to cast ballots for a crucial Senate election.

Voting-rights advocates in Missouri are arguing in court that the state underfunded efforts to educate residents on a voter ID law. In North Carolina, the legislature's regulation of early-voting hours has shuttered polling places across the state, even as it purports to increase voting opportunities.

Nathaniel Persily, a Stanford University law professor and elections scholar, said what was going on reflected a shift from a belief in shared rules of democracy toward one that sees elections as struggles for power "in which you need to push up against the rules to win."

He added, "We've reached a situation in which the fight over the rules and who gets to vote is seen as a legitimate part of electoral competition."

Republicans consistently say restrictions on registering and voting are needed to combat election fraud, a view most prominently expressed in President Trump's widely derided statement, with no evidence, that millions of illegal voters cost him the popular vote in 2016. Studies regularly conclude that fraud is exceedingly rare; a New York Times survey of 49 state election offices after the 2016 general election found no allegations of widespread fraud, and no fraud claims at all in 26 states.

But even within the Republican Party there is not universal agreement. The Texas secretary of state, Rolando Pablos, a Republican, sent a letter Tuesday asking Waller County to extend early voting at Prairie View's campus polling site throughout the week. The county resisted, however.

It added a single day of additional voting off-campus after the lawsuit was filed, and some additional hours on campus, but a top official said it did not have the resources or time to do more.

For Mr. Johnson, an independent, getting to other polling sites is difficult. He has a full class schedule to balance with several chemistry and business clubs, and he lives off campus, without a car.

"If I'm not eating or sleeping or studying, I'm really in class or in a meeting," he said after voting Tuesday at the student center, outfitted with a backpack and a bandanna.

He expressed satisfaction that even a single day of voting had been added, but expected disputes to continue because, as he put it, "we might not vote the way they want us to vote."

While restrictions are on the rise in some states, others have made it easier to vote.

In the last three years alone, 15 states have moved to automatically register voters (unless they opt out) when they visit motor-vehicle agencies. Colorado, Washington and Oregon now allow all voters to cast ballots by mail, while 37 states and the District of Columbia let voters cast ballots early. Florida voters will decide next week whether to end the disenfranchisement of felons, while 23 states have already loosened similar policies. Six million Americans with felony convictions still cannot cast ballots.

Some experts say that even intentional suppression, while contrary to democratic elections, is not likely to have a huge impact on vote totals.

"The estimates you get are that these sorts of changes might reduce turnout by a percentage point or two," said Charles Stewart III, an expert on election administration at the Massachusetts Institute of Technology.

But with dozens of congressional and governor's races now within the margin of polling error, a point or two could easily decide many races — with control of Congress at stake.

Several court rulings say Republicans increasingly are writing voting rules with partisan intent. Voter ID legislation in Texas labels gun licenses acceptable at polling places, but not college identifications. Arizona has made it a crime to collect absentee ballots for transport to a voting site, a staple get-out-the-vote practice.

Nearly a thousand polling places have been closed nationwide in the last half-decade, according to a recent Pew report. And the number of people being purged from voter rolls is rising sharply, according to a Brennan Center study. Another study by the center last year counted at least 99 bills introduced in 31 states to restrict voting access.

States routinely cull their lists of registered voters of those who have died or moved away, but some purge so aggressively that they sweep up legitimate voters. Ohio's policy, upheld this year by the Supreme Court, is the strictest: Voters who skip a single election receive a postcard warning them that they are being marked inactive. If they don't return the card and then don't vote in the two succeeding elections, they are removed from the rolls.

Such policies can have a profound effect. If Ohio's policy had been applied in Florida and North Carolina, 89,000 people who voted in 2016 would have been disenfranchised, according to an analysis by Daniel A. Smith of the University of Florida and Michael C. Herron of Dartmouth College.

"It's shocking," Dr. Smith said. "We don't ask gun owners to fire their weapons every two years and revoke their licenses four years later if they don't."

Some voters are pushing back.

"It's frustrating that young voters are told that they are shameful for not voting, and then when we ask for measures that ensure we can vote, we are often mocked," said Megan Newsome, 22, a recent graduate of the University of Florida who fought successfully to bring voting back to Florida campuses, and was a plaintiff in a suit against Florida's secretary of state.

Both parties have something to gain, depending on a larger or smaller electorate.

Traditionally, Democrats do better with a larger electorate, leading Republicans to fight such measures as the 1993 "motor-voter" law that let Americans register at driver-license and public assistance offices. A number of conservative advocacy groups have sprung up in recent years, bankrolling efforts to challenge voter registrations, and are a counterweight to civil rights groups and legal organizations like the American Civil Liberties Union.

"The people that are being quote unquote purged, are dead, usually about 40 percent of the time," said Logan C. Churchwell, the communications and research director at the Public Interest Legal Foundation, one such group. "The remainder of them are relocated out of the jurisdiction and long gone, or felons. You're not talking about someone who hasn't moved and are still kicking and breathing," adding, "You can't silence a dead guy."

But thousands of voters who wanted to vote, and who have not moved, have been struck from voter rolls in high-profile incidents from Brooklyn to Georgia to Ohio.

The two secretaries of state most aggressive in culling voter lists are Kris Kobach in Kansas and Brian Kemp in Georgia, who are also both Republican candidates for governor, exacerbating partisan rancor. Mr. Kemp has presided over a series of purges and restrictive voter-registration rules that heavily affect minorities. Mr. Kemp is white, and his Democratic opponent, Stacey Abrams, is black.

"Voter suppression isn't only about blocking the vote, it's also about creating an atmosphere of fear, making people worry that their votes won't count," Ms. Abrams said at a recent debate.

Mr. Kemp has expressed unease at Democratic turnout, but called suggestions of suppression "outrageous" and said that over all "we have one million more people on our voting rolls" than when he took office in 2010. But he had a setback Friday when a federal judge ruled that Georgia needed to make it less difficult for naturalized citizens to vote.

For Waller County, voter suppression has weighed on its reputation. It was further tarnished in 2015, when Sandra Bland, a Prairie View alumna, who was heading back to the school to take a job, was the subject of a highly controversial police stop and subsequent jailing that ended with her suicide.

Officials defend the county.

"I got to Waller County in '05, so every time every story starts with Waller County and its 40-year racist history of disenfranchising voters, I have no connection to that at all," said Judge Carbett J. Duhon III, a Republican who is the top official setting voting rules.

"Hindsight being 20/20, can I understand students being frustrated that maybe they are excited for one candidate or the other, and they don't have a place to go vote on campus during that first week?" he asked. "Yeah, I can see that."

DANNY HAKIM reported from Prairie View, Tex., and **MICHAEL WINES** from Washington.

Before the Fights Over Recounts: An Election Day Vote on Voting

BY DANNY HAKIM | NOV. 12, 2018

AMID THE RECOUNTS, recriminations and allegations of voter suppression or ballot fraud, something else happened in Tuesday's elections — a wave of actions aimed at making voting easier and fairer that is an often-overlooked strain in the nation's voting wars.

Floridians extended voting rights to 1.4 million convicted felons. Maryland, Nevada and Michigan were among states that made it easier to register and vote. Michigan, along with Colorado and Missouri, limited politicians' ability to directly draw, and gerrymander, district lines. Utah, where votes are still being tallied, appears poised to do the same.

It was as if states around the country were pulled in two directions at once — with measures aimed at broadening voter participation coming on the heels of recent laws and regulations making it harder to register and vote.

Still, for all the charges and countercharges on voter suppression, most of the momentum Tuesday was on measures quite likely to broaden voter participation and limit gerrymanders.

"It is clear when you put democracy reforms on the ballot, those measures win overwhelmingly," Karen Hobert Flynn, president of Common Cause, said. "From our perspective, we are going to be taking a hard look at where we can move more of these reforms in 2020 and beyond."

There was plenty of news in the other direction, most notably the potential for prolonged legal fights over tight races in Florida, Georgia and Arizona. Many Americans cast ballots whose weight was diluted by precise, data-driven gerrymanders. North Carolina and Arkansas bucked this year's voter-friendly tide by creating new identification requirements.

Sometimes, clashing electoral policies played out within the same state. While Floridians voted to re-enfranchise felons, college students there had to fend off a move by Florida's secretary of state to bar voting on campus. In Michigan, voters reinstated straight-ticket voting, which makes it easy to quickly vote for a single party across elections, overturning a move by the Republican-controlled legislature in 2015 to abolish it.

Nationwide, the varying moves are the latest chapter in an escalating battle between Democrats, who tend to gain with a larger electorate, and Republicans, whose policies often push in the opposite direction.

How Americans vote is likely to remain on the front burner as both parties turn toward the 2020 presidential year elections. Arnold Schwarzenegger, a backer of redistricting reform — he has a Terminate Gerrymandering PAC — said last week he will seek to build on recent gains and hold a summit on the topic.

The election was also a reminder that, despite episodes of voter suppression, substantial progress is being made at increasing turnout, which was at the highest rate for a midterm in more than half a century. While the polarization and passion of the Trump era was likely the primary reason, the ease of early voting and automatic registration contributed. For the most part, the array of new ballot measures were aimed at continuing to make voting easier.

That reflects the way voting issues combine both deeply political impulses and largely practical ones.

"There are voting reforms which trigger partisan sensibilities, and then there are those that respond to people's desire to have a modern, efficient and nonbureaucratic process," said Nathaniel Persily, a Stanford University law professor and elections scholar. "People want options. They don't want to be forced to go to a polling place; they want to be able to vote from home. Right now, when people can conduct their entire lives on their phone, they wonder why they have to go to a 19th century polling place to cast a ballot."

Several of the measures sparked partisan battles, like Michigan's Proposal 2, which created a commission to draw district lines, and Issue 2 in Arkansas, which requires voters to have photo identification and was opposed by the American Civil Liberties Union.

The A.C.L.U. also targeted Kris Kobach, the Kansas secretary of state and candidate for governor who became a villain among liberals after repeatedly making spurious claims about widespread voter fraud. While the A.C.L.U. does not officially endorse or oppose specific candidates, it made its feelings clear in Mr. Kobach's race, with a $400,000 TV ad buy, 150,000 mailers, 70,000 phone calls and by knocking on more than 5,000 doors. Mr. Kobach lost.

"When voters — actual people — get an opportunity to shape their election system, it's unequivocal where they are, but when it's politicians who are rendering judgment of the system, they are protecting the status quo and engineering outcomes to their advantage," Faiz Shakir, national political director of the A.C.L.U., said. "The main lesson here is that we should go big and bold on voting rights."

The group was a central player in many of the progressive ballot measures, and it projected that, taken together, they will expand voting rights to two million people.

Conservatives say that what Americans most want is an electorate in which everyone has been found to be eligible to vote.

Donald Bryson, the chief executive of Civitas Institute, a Raleigh-based conservative policy group, said North Carolina voters backed the state's voter ID measure because it "brings security to the electoral process." Civitas has opposed steps like allowing voters to register on Election Day, as Maryland did. Mr. Bryson said same-day registration could "make voters nervous about the integrity of the election, and that is something we should be wary of."

Some of the highest-profile initiatives were less partisan than one might expect.

Republicans generally did not contest reinstating voting rights to Florida felons, even though demographics suggest the change is likely to favor Democrats. The Brennan Center called it "the largest expansion of voting rights" since the 26th Amendment lowered the voting age to 18 in 1971.

The biggest financial backers of the Florida effort, by far, were the A.C.L.U. and one of the so-called "dark money" groups that have proliferated on both sides of the aisle. Combined, the A.C.L.U. and the Sixteen Thirty Fund, a left-leaning group, donated more than $9 million of the $10.2 million budget of the Floridians for a Fair Democracy, the group of former felons and family members that led the effort.

While Florida Governor Rick Scott and Ron DeSantis, the Republican candidates for Senate and governor, expressed measured opposition, many Republicans supported the measure.

"A significant number of folks voted straight red and pulled for the amendment," said Logan C. Churchwell, the communications and research director at the Public Interest Legal Foundation, a conservative group that wants states to aggressively cull their voter rolls.

"Some people interpret felon voting rights like any other question of redemption," he added in an email. "Federalism at play here."

The effort was also endorsed by Freedom Partners, backed by the Koch brothers, conservative stalwarts; the group said that "when individuals have served their sentences and paid their debts as ordered by a judge, they should be eligible to vote." The A.C.L.U. and Freedom Partners even sent out a joint mailer.

"I'm not 180 degrees changing my position on the Koch brothers, but I did take note of it," said Miles Rapoport, a senior fellow at Harvard University and a Democrat who is the former secretary of state of Connecticut. "It will transform Florida's politics."

Mr. Rapoport was encouraged both by the preponderance of progressive ballot measures and the shifting control in statehouses in some key states, like New York, where Democrats captured the State Senate, the only wing of the government they lacked, and North Carolina, where Republicans lost their supermajority. Unlike most states, New York does not allow early voting.

"There will be a lot of places to watch where there will be opportunities for further reform," Mr. Rapoport said.

Officials in Colorado, which created two commissions to take over the task of drawing district lines, went even further in finding bipartisan compromise.

Frank McNulty, the former Republican Speaker of the state's House of Representatives, said the political parties essentially called an armistice, setting aside their own ballot measures on redistricting.

"There was an agreement that there would be a laying down of arms," Mr. McNulty said. "It was one of those things that we did to build trust."

Mark Grueskin, a prominent Colorado lawyer who was the lead negotiator for the Democrats, said "each side has to have a serious motivating factor to be at the table."

He added: "My sense is that the demographics of the voting populations in each state are going to determine how willing those states are to nurture the possibility of an open election process."

Some did not even get to vote on ballot measures that will change their lives.

Neil Volz, the political director of the Floridians for a Fair Democracy, has a felony conviction related to the Jack Abramoff lobbying scandal.

"We were crying and hugging," Mr. Volz, a Republican, said of winning back his right to vote. "We're fighting just as hard for people who want to vote for Donald Trump as we are for people who want to vote for Barack Obama."

House Passes Democrats' Centerpiece Anti-Corruption and Voting Rights Bill

BY CATIE EDMONDSON | MARCH 8, 2019

WASHINGTON — The House passed the Democrats' showcase anti-corruption and voting rights legislation on Friday, an expansive measure that aims to dismantle barriers to the ballot box, end big money in politics and impose stricter ethics rules on federal officials.

The sweeping legislation, passed 234-193, makes good on the campaign pledge to clean up Washington that helped catapult Democrats into the majority. It also serves as a campaign platform for Democrats ahead of 2020. It has virtually no chance of passing the Senate.

"It's a power grab for the American people," said Representative Zoe Lofgren of California, who leads the House administration committee that shepherded the legislation.

The ambitious compendium, at nearly 700 pages, includes proposals automatically registering citizens to vote and restoring voting rights to people who have served felony sentences. It also creates a six-to-one matching system for donations of up to $200 to congressional and presidential candidates who reject high-dollar contributions, funded by an additional fine on corporations found to have broken the law.

Republicans arguably have spent more time trying to define the bill — called the For the People Act or H.R. 1, to underscore its primacy — and tear it down than Democrats have spent trying to promote it. Senator Mitch McConnell of Kentucky, the majority leader, has branded it the "Democrat Politician Protection Act" in weekly speeches, and pledged not to take up the legislation. The House Republican leader, Representative Kevin McCarthy of California, also criticized the legislation.

"This bill is a massive federal government takeover that would undermine the integrity of our elections," Mr. McCarthy said in a speech on Friday, in an attack on "this new, Democrat, socialist majority."

Speaker Nancy Pelosi and House members spoke on the steps of the Capitol on Friday about the For the People Act.

Some of the most debated provisions are intended to reveal who funds online political ads and finances so-called dark-money groups. The Disclose Act, part of the bill, would require super PACs and non-profit organizations that spend money in elections to disclose the names of donors who contribute more than $10,000. Democrats say such disclosure is broadly popular with voters across the political spectrum.

"Congress cannot meaningfully address the nation's significant challenges without first recognizing and acknowledging the undue influence of special interests in our politics," said Representative Abigail Spanberger, Democrat of Virginia.

Some of those provisions, however, have drawn criticism from both conservative and liberal groups that argue the language is overly broad and would infringe on First Amendment rights. The American Civil Liberties Union urged members to vote against the bill.

Democrats have also used the legislation to make clear that they believe that cleanup must start with the White House, and included several provisions jabbing at the president and homing in on a laundry list of his administration's alleged ethical abuses.

It would require presidents and vice presidents, as well as candidates for the nation's highest offices, to release at least 10 years of federal tax returns — Mr. Trump has released none — and it stipulates that inaugural committees must disclose their expenditures.

And an amendment sponsored by Representative Raul Ruiz of California would prohibit federal funds from being spent at businesses owned or controlled by the president, the vice president or any cabinet official. Federal agencies spent about $13 million on four of Mr. Trump's trips to his Mar-a-Lago resort in Florida in early 2017, according to a report by a nonpartisan congressional watchdog agency issued last month.

Two other measures also zero in on the costs of administration officials' travel. One provision would require the Defense Department to regularly report to Congress details of the costs of presidential travel; the other would prohibit political appointees from using federal funds to pay for travel on noncommercial or private flights for official business.

"We must hold our government leaders to the highest standards, and with so many high-profile ethics violations in the past years, it is clear we have failed to do that," Representative Tom O'Halleran, Democrat of Arizona and the sponsor of the amendments, said in a statement.

Democrats also successfully put down an attempt by Republicans to divide the caucus and tar the legislation with a resolution expressing the sense that "allowing illegal immigrants the right to vote devalues the franchise and diminishes the voting power of United States citizens."

Republicans have repeatedly ambushed Democrats — twice successfully — with politically freighted procedural motions in a drive to divide Democrats and draw out vulnerable swing-district members. But determined not to let that taint their signature legislation and fired up by a rousing speech from freshman Representative Max Rose of New York, Democrats held steady.

House Passes Voting Rights Bill Despite Near Unanimous Republican Opposition

BY SHERYL GAY STOLBERG AND EMILY COCHRANE | DEC. 6, 2019

The legislation restores the core of the Voting Rights Act, the landmark civil rights statute to guard against racial discrimination in elections.

WASHINGTON — The House voted on Friday to reinstate federal oversight of state election law, moving to bolster protections against racial discrimination enshrined in the 1965 Voting Rights Act, the landmark civil rights statute whose central provision was struck down by the Supreme Court.

Representative John Lewis, Democrat of Georgia, who was beaten in 1965 while demonstrating for voting rights in Alabama, banged the gavel to herald approval of the measure, to applause from his colleagues on the House floor. It passed by a vote of 228 to 187 nearly along party lines, with all but one Republican opposed.

The bill has little chance of becoming law given opposition in the Republican-controlled Senate and by President Trump, whose aides issued a veto threat against it this week.

The measure is a direct response to the 2013 Supreme Court decision in the case of Shelby County v. Holder, in which the justices invalidated a key portion of the law. They asserted that the federal oversight of elections was no longer necessary in nine states, mostly in the South, because of strides made in advancing voting rights since passage of the 1965 law.

The original Voting Rights Act, signed by President Lyndon B. Johnson as a centerpiece of his civil rights agenda, was meant to bar states from imposing poll taxes, literacy tests and other methods to keep black people from voting. Democrats argued that while such overt barriers are gone, they have been replaced by stricter voting laws adopted by 25 states since the Shelby decision.

"Selma is still now!" thundered Representative Terri A. Sewell, Democrat of Alabama, the chief sponsor of the measure, during debate on the measure on the floor. "I know I'm not the only black and brown colleague of ours who owes their very presence in this chamber to the Voting Rights Act passed in 1965."

Republicans, for their part, argued that the bill would trample on states' ability to dictate their own election rules by abusing measures in place to prevent voter disenfranchisement.

"The bill before us today would turn those federal shields that protect voters into political weapons," said Representative Doug Collins of Georgia, the top Republican on the House Judiciary Committee, adding that the legislation would do so "when there is absolutely no evidence whatsoever that those states or localities engaged in any discriminatory behavior when it comes to voting."

The debate underscored the deep partisan polarization that has taken hold on issues related to voting and elections in recent years. In 2006, the last time the Voting Rights Act was updated, the measure passed overwhelmingly in the House, where large majorities of both parties supported it, unanimously passed the Senate, and was signed into law by a Republican president, George W. Bush.

On Friday, just one Republican, Representative Brian Fitzpatrick of Pennsylvania, voted "yes."

In the Shelby case, Chief Justice John G. Roberts Jr. wrote that Congress remained free to try to impose federal oversight on states where voting rights were at risk, but must do so based on contemporary data. The measure passed on Friday was an attempt to do just that.

Specifically, it would update the parameters used to determine which states and territories need to seek approval for electoral procedures, requiring public notice for voting changes and expanding access for Native American and Alaska Native voters.

But it is unlikely to come to a vote in the Senate, where Senator Mitch McConnell, Republican of Kentucky and the majority leader, has refused to take up most legislation championed by House Democrats.

Still, Democrats saw its passage as a significant victory and an important statement of their principles — as well as evidence that they can legislate while also preparing articles of impeachment against President Trump.

With the number of legislative days in the year dwindling into the single digits, Democrats are rushing as much work as they can across the House floor to keep the government running and maximize a record of accomplishments they can show voters before the 2020 elections.

H.R. 4, formally titled the Voting Rights Advancement Act and given a low number by Democrats to reflect its priority on their agenda, was the product of a series of hearings in eight states and Washington, as well as hours of testimony. Black Democrats and those who are old enough to remember the debate over the 1965 bill spoke about the new legislation with passion — and a sense of history.

"I have been thinking a lot this morning about my growing up in South Carolina," said Representative James E. Clyburn, 79, the No. 3 House Democrat, describing how he drove to a tiny town in his native state to see the Rev. Dr. Martin Luther King Jr. speak, just a few months after Johnson signed the 1965 bill into law.

"I'll never forget his theme that day: March to the ballot box," Mr. Clyburn said.

SHERYL GAY STOLBERG covers Congress, focusing on domestic policy. She has been a national correspondent, political features writer and White House correspondent and shared in two Pulitzer Prizes at The Los Angeles Times.

EMILY COCHRANE is a reporter in the Washington bureau, covering Congress. She was raised in Miami and graduated from the University of Florida.

Attacking the 'Woke' Black Vote

OPINION | BY CHARLES M. BLOW | FEB. 18, 2018

ONE THING THAT is clear to me following the special counsel's indictment of 13 Russians and three companies for interfering with our election is that the black vote was specifically under attack, from sources foreign and domestic. And this attack appeared to be particularly focused on young black activist-minded voters passionate about social justice: The "Woke" Vote.

The tragic irony is that these young people, many of whom already felt like the American political system was failing them, were encouraged to lay down one of the most powerful political tools they have, thereby ensuring an amplification of their own oppressions.

The indictment proclaims that the defendants acted as Americans to create social media pages and groups "which addressed divisive U.S. political and social issues." But that is a phrase so broad and bland as to obscure the piercing truth that the indictment reveals: Referencing actual voter suppression, it says that "in or around the latter half of 2016, Defendants and their co-conspirators, through their personas, began to encourage U.S. minority groups not to vote in the 2016 U.S. presidential election or to vote for a third-party U.S. presidential candidate."

Indeed, the indictment includes some examples of that effort to suppress:

"On or about October 16, 2016, Defendants and their co-conspirators used the Instagram account 'Woke Blacks' to post the following message: 'Particular hype and hatred for Trump is misleading the people and forcing Blacks to vote Killary. We cannot resort to the lesser of two devils. Then we'd surely be better off without voting AT ALL.' " Coincidentally (or not!) this was the exact same tack being taken by the Trump campaign during that time. Just before the election, a senior Trump campaign official told Bloomberg Businessweek, "We have three major voter suppression operations under way," in which Hillary Clinton's "1996 suggestion that some African-American males are 'super predators' is the basis of a below-the-radar effort to discourage infrequent black voters from showing up at the polls — particularly in Florida." This suppression may well have worked better against black people than other targets.

According to a May Pew Research Center report, "The black voter turnout rate declined for the first time in 20 years in a presidential election." The report said that the number of naturalized citizen voters was up from 2012 and the turnout rate for women was mostly unchanged from 2012.

And while the percentage of eligible millennials who said they voted in the last election rose among every other demographic group, it fell among black millennials.

Trump even had the audacity during one of his thank you rallies to laud his voter suppression efforts and thank black voters for not voting:

"They didn't come out to vote for Hillary. They didn't come out. And that was a big — so thank you to the African-American community."

Now, it can surely be argued that the numbers for women and other minorities might have been even higher had it not been for the suppressive efforts, but at least their turnout numbers didn't decline. For black people, they did. It is entirely possible that many, if not most of, the black people who decided not to vote in this election would have done so even without Trump and Russian prodding. Also, President Obama wasn't on the ballot.

Indeed, early in the primaries, Michelle Alexander, author of the acclaimed book "The New Jim Crow" — which has attained near Bible stature among some social justice activists — laid out a strong philosophical argument for "why Hillary Clinton doesn't deserve the black vote." It hinged largely on crime and economic policies enacted when Bill Clinton was president, policies Hillary then supported.

Even after Clinton accepted the Democratic nomination, rapper Killer Mike, a prominent Bernie Sanders supporter and surrogate, was still promoting the position that "If you're voting for Trump or Hillary Clinton, you're voting for the same thing."

On Election Day, many young black people held their noses and voted, commenting on social media with the hashtag #IGuessImWithHer. But many simply abstained. Shortly after the election, The Sacramento Bee pointed out that Colin Kaepernick, now lionized as a social justice hero, had never registered to vote in any election. When asked why he didn't vote in even the recent presidential election, the football player responded:

"I said from the beginning I was against oppression, I was against the system of oppression. I'm not going to show support for that system. And to me, the oppressor isn't going to allow you to vote your way out of your oppression." To the contrary, it has been the triple threats of voting, legislation and court rulings, all set against the backdrop of direct action, that has inched America forward. But it is each American's right to do with the vote what he or she chooses, including withholding it.

There is no way to know how many black people would have settled on the exact same course of action without the interference. But what we do now know with absolute certainty is that in making their electoral choices, black folks had unwanted hands on their backs, unethical and illegal ones, nudging them toward an apathy built on anger.

What happened in this election wasn't just a political crime, it was specifically a racialized crime, and the black vote was a central target.

CHARLES M. BLOW has been a New York Times Op-Ed columnist since 2008.

Russian Efforts Exploited Racial Divisions, State of Black America Report Says

BY MIHIR ZAVERI AND JACEY FORTIN | MAY 6, 2019

RUSSIAN DISINFORMATION OPERATIONS to exploit racial tensions during the 2016 presidential election in the United States found firm ground in a country where legislators have long sought to suppress the black vote, according to a report released Monday.

The report, "State of Black America," was released by the National Urban League, a civil rights organization based in New York. It underlined the Russian interference in particular but said that black voting rights were under attack from a wide range of actors, including domestic politicians.

In about two dozen states, voting restrictions have gotten worse since 2010 because of changes including new voter identification laws and decisions to limit locations where voters can cast ballots, the report said.

The report's findings on the Russian interference drew from academic research and federal investigations to highlight the huge campaign run by a St. Petersburg company called the Internet Research Agency, which deployed thousands of accounts on Facebook, Twitter and other platforms.

One such account on Twitter, called @WokeLuisa, garnered more than 50,000 followers, and its posts were highlighted by dozens of prominent news outlets, the report said.

The account sought to explicitly and implicitly discourage black voters from going to the polls in an effort to secure Republican victory, even as other Russian-backed efforts bolstered white extremism online, said Marc H. Morial, the president of the National Urban League.

"It was targeted, it was focused," Mr. Morial said. "It's intentionally pouring gasoline on racial division."

The F.B.I. has warned that the threat of Russian interference in American elections persists. Intelligence officials have said that Russia interfered throughout the midterm elections last year, and that those efforts are likely to intensify during the next presidential campaign.

Bret Schafer, the social media analyst at the Alliance for Securing Democracy, an initiative to combat efforts to undermine democratic institutions that is housed at the German Marshall Fund of the United States, wrote about the Russian interference in the report and described @WokeLuisa as one of many fake accounts that impersonated African-American people to exploit pre-existing animosity and discourage voting.

"It's moving the dial just a couple of degrees in the direction they want it to go," Mr. Schafer said in an interview. "The anonymity of the internet allows you to be whoever you want to be, and of course you're going to be far more persuasive if that target audience thinks you're one of them."

The report also outlined domestic efforts to both empower and disenfranchise minority voters.

Citing data compiled by the Brennan Center for Justice, the report said that as of March, more than 40 states had passed or were considering bills expanding access to voting, for instance by easing the voter registration process, expanding early voting and giving voting rights to convicted felons.

But domestic restrictions on voting, the vast majority of which are imposed by Republicans, proliferated in many states, the report found. Such moves reflect rising partisanship, societal shifts toward greater diversity, and the weakening of the Voting Rights Act by the Supreme Court in 2013.

Mr. Morial said it was not possible to disentangle the Russian interference campaign from other factors that determined black voter turnout in the 2016 election, since both involved racial targeting.

Joel Ford, a former Democratic state senator in North Carolina who was a sponsor of a voter identification bill there, disagreed. "I think that those are two separate issues," he said. "One is something that we as Americans can control through the legislative process, and the other is foreign interference in our elections."

Mr. Ford said that as an African-American man, he was sensitive to discriminatory voter suppression tactics. But he called blanket opposition to voter identification laws "an unnecessary political wedge," in part because it is a state-by-state issue, and laws can be crafted to minimize discrimination.

He added that photo identification was already necessary for activities like banking or flying, and that the bill he supported in North Carolina allowed voters to obtain photo identification cards at no cost. (That bill passed in December after the Legislature overrode the Democratic governor's veto. Monday's report named North Carolina as one of the states where voting restrictions have gotten worse.)

The report, which is now in its 43rd annual edition, featured more than 30 other essays written by various authors including scholars, politicians and corporate executives.

It also recommended a number of policy changes, including automatic voter registration, the creation of a national commission to "identify and eliminate foreign interference in the American democratic process," and postelection auditing to compare paper ballots to computerized tabulations.

And Mr. Morial said he hoped Congress would hold hearings on Russian efforts to target black voters.

"I tell people: Russia today, China tomorrow, Saudi Arabia next week," he said. "Every country that wants to influence and impact us is going to be playing in our elections."

Glossary

absentee ballot A mechanism for people to vote if they will be out of town or otherwise unable to vote in person on Election Day.

disenfranchisement The state of blocking a person or group's right to vote.

early voting An established process allowing people to cast a ballot ahead of Election Day. Methods for doing so vary by state; not all states allow it.

election fraud Illegal interference in the process of an election so as to ensure one candidate's election.

felon A person convicted of a serious, usually violent crime.

in-person voter fraud Illegal interference in the process of an election by individual people who pretend to be someone else at the polls.

poll tax A fee required in order to register to vote or to cast a ballot. Such taxes were outlawed by the Twenty-fourth Amendment to the U.S. Constitution in 1964.

precinct A district divided out for administrative purposes, such as the administration of an election.

turnout The number of eligible people who vote in an election.

voter identification (ID) law A law that requires voters to present an approved form of identification (often including a photo) in order to vote. These laws and their requirements vary by state.

voter intimidation Pressure on or fear induced in voters either to convince them to vote for a certain candidate, or to prevent them from voting at all.

Media Literacy Terms

"Media literacy" refers to the ability to access, understand, critically assess and create media. The following terms are important components of media literacy, and they will help you critically engage with the articles in this title.

angle The aspect of a news story that a journalist focuses on and develops.

attribution The method by which a source is identified or by which facts and information are assigned to the person who provided them.

balance Principle of journalism that both perspectives of an argument should be presented in a fair way.

bias A disposition of prejudice in favor of a certain idea, person or perspective.

credibility The quality of being trustworthy and believable, said of a journalistic source.

commentary A type of story that is an expression of opinion on recent events by a journalist generally known as a commentator.

credibility The quality of being trustworthy and believable, said of a journalistic source.

critical review A type of story that describes an event or work of art, such as a theater performance, film, concert, book, restaurant, radio or television program, exhibition or musical piece, and offers critical assessment of its quality and reception.

editorial Article of opinion or interpretation.

headline Type, usually 18 point or larger, used to introduce a story.

impartiality Principle of journalism that a story should not reflect a journalist's bias and should contain balance.

intention The motive or reason behind something, such as the publication of a news story.

motive The reason behind something, such as the publication of a news story or a source's perspective on an issue.

news story An article or style of expository writing that reports news, generally in a straightforward fashion and without editorial comment.

op-ed An opinion piece that reflects a prominent individual's opinion on a topic of interest.

paraphrase The summary of an individual's words, with attribution, rather than a direct quotation of their exact words.

plagiarism An attempt to pass another person's work as one's own without attribution.

quotation The use of an individual's exact words indicated by the use of quotation marks and proper attribution.

reliability The quality of being dependable and accurate, said of a journalistic source.

rhetorical device Technique in writing intending to persuade the reader or communicate a message from a certain perspective.

source The origin of the information reported in journalism.

style A distinctive use of language in writing or speech; also a news or publishing organization's rules for consistent use of language with regard to spelling, punctuation, typography and capitalization, usually regimented by a house style guide.

tone A manner of expression in writing or speech.

Media Literacy
Questions

1. "Whose Votes Really Count?" (on page 30) is an example of a critical review. What is the purpose of a critical review? Do you feel this article achieved that purpose?

2. Identify the various sources cited in the article "The Student Vote Is Surging. So Are Efforts to Suppress It." (on page 34). How does Michael Wines attribute information to each of the sources in his article? How effective are his attributions in helping the reader identify his sources?

3. Compare the headlines of "Maine Republicans Want to Get There (Vote Suppression) From Here (Vote Turnout)" (on page 63) and "The Republicans' Obsession With Voter Suppression" (on page 65). Which is a more compelling headline, and why? How could the less compelling headline be changed to better draw the reader's interest?

4. Often, as a news story develops, a journalist's attitude toward the subject may change. Compare "Some Republicans Acknowledge Leveraging Voter ID Laws for Political Gain" (on page 67) and "Asked for Voters' Data, States Give Trump Panel a Bipartisan 'No' " (on page 83), both by Michael Wines. Did new information discovered between the publication of these two articles change Wines's perspective?

5. What is the intention of the article "Questions and Answers on Voter Fraud" (on page 72)? How effectively does it achieve its intended purpose?

6. Does William Neuman demonstrate the journalistic principle of balance in his article "400,000 New Yorkers Were Told Their Voter Registrations Were Inactive. Oops." (on page 120)? If so, how did he do so? If not, what could he have included to make his article more balanced?

7. The article "Stacey Abrams: We Cannot Resign Ourselves to Dismay and Disenfranchisement" (on page 159) is an example of an op-ed. Identify how Stacey Abrams's attitude and tone help convey her opinion on the topic.

8. "How Voter Suppression Could Swing the Midterms" (on page 183) features a chart. What does this chart add to the article?

9. Does "Russian Efforts Exploited Racial Divisions, State of Black America Report Says" (on page 209) use multiple sources? What are the strengths of using multiple sources in a journalistic piece? What are the weaknesses of relying heavily on only one or a few sources?

Citations

All citations in this list are formatted according to the Modern Language Association's (MLA) style guide.

BOOK CITATION

THE NEW YORK TIMES EDITORIAL STAFF. *Voter Suppression: Blocking the Ballot Box*. New York Times Educational Publishing, 2021.

ONLINE ARTICLE CITATIONS

ABRAMS, STACEY. "Stacey Abrams: We Cannot Resign Ourselves to Dismay and Disenfranchisement." *The New York Times*, 15 May 2019, https://www.nytimes.com/2019/05/15/opinion/stacey-abrams-voting.html.

AHTONE, TRISTAN. "Democrats, Don't Take Native American Voters for Granted." *The New York Times*, 29 Oct. 2018, https://www.nytimes.com/2018/10/29/opinion/north-dakota-senate-native-american-voters.html.

BAZELON, EMILY. "The Supreme Court Rule That Voting Restrictions Were a Bygone Problem. Early Voting Results Suggest Otherwise." *The New York Times*, 7 Nov. 2016, https://www.nytimes.com/2016/11/07/magazine/the-supreme-court-ruled-that-voting-restrictions-were-a-bygone-problem-early-voting-results-suggest-otherwise.html.

BERMAN, ARI. "How Voter Suppression Could Swing the Midterms." *The New York Times*, 27 Oct. 2018, https://www.nytimes.com/2018/10/27/opinion/sunday/voter-suppression-georgia-2018.html.

BLINDER, ALAN. "Questions and Answers on Voter Fraud." *The New York Times*, 5 Aug. 2016, https://www.nytimes.com/2016/08/05/us/voter-id-laws-donald-trump.html.

BLINDER, ALAN, AND RICHARD FAUSSET. "Stacey Abrams Ends Fight for Georgia Governor With Harsh Words for Her Rival." *The New York Times*, 16 Nov. 2018, https://www.nytimes.com/2018/11/16/us/elections/georgia-governor-race-kemp-abrams.html.

BLINDER, ALAN, AND MICHAEL WINES. "Black Turnout in Alabama Complicates Debate on Voting Laws." *The New York Times*, 24 Dec. 2017, https://www.nytimes.com/2017/12/24/us/alabama-voting-blacks-.html.

BLOW, CHARLES M. "Attacking the 'Woke' Black Vote." *The New York Times*, 2 Feb. 2018, https://www.nytimes.com/2018/02/18/opinion/black-vote-russia.html.

BROWN, ELISHA. "Federal Judge Backs Georgia's Purge of Nearly 100,000 Voters." *The New York Times*, 27 Dec. 2019, https://www.nytimes.com/2019/12/27/us/elections/georgia-voters-purge.html.

BURCH, AUDRA D. S. "A New Class of Voting Rights Activists Picks Up the Mantle in Mississippi." *The New York Times*, 25 Sept. 2018, https://www.nytimes.com/2018/09/25/us/freedom-summer-mississippi-votes.html.

CHOKSHI, NIRAJ. "How to Report Voter Intimidation, and How to Spot It." *The New York Times*, 6 Nov. 2018, https://www.nytimes.com/2018/11/06/us/politics/reporting-voter-intimidation.html.

CLINES, FRANCIS X. "The Republicans' Obsession With Voter Suppression." *The New York Times*, 20 May 2016, https://takingnote.blogs.nytimes.com/2016/05/20/the-republicans-obsession-with-voter-suppression/.

COHN, NATE. "Why Voter ID Laws Don't Swing Many Elections." *The New York Times*, 20 Nov. 2014, https://www.nytimes.com/2014/11/20/upshot/why-voter-id-laws-dont-swing-many-elections.html.

DAVEY, MONICA, AND MITCH SMITH. "Wisconsin Judge Says State Must Purge 200,000 Voter Registrations." *The New York Times*, 19 Dec. 2019, https://www.nytimes.com/2019/12/13/us/wisconsin-voter-rolls-purge.html.

DAVIS, JULIE HIRSCHFELD. "Trump Picks Voter ID Advocate for Election Fraud Panel." *The New York Times*, 11 May 2017, https://www.nytimes.com/2017/05/11/us/politics/trump-voter-fraud.html.

DOUTHAT, ROSS. "The Myths of Voter ID." *The New York Times*, 12 Feb. 2019, https://www.nytimes.com/2019/02/12/opinion/voter-id-study-republicans-democrats.html.

EDMONDSON, CATIE. "House Passes Democrats' Centerpiece Anti-Corruption and Voting Rights Bill." *The New York Times*, 8 Mar. 2019, https://www.nytimes.com/2019/03/08/us/politics/house-democrats-anticorruption-voting-rights.html.

FAUSSET, RICHARD. "Georgia County Rejects Plan to Close 7 Polling Places in Majority-Black Area." *The New York Times*, 23 Aug. 2018, https://www.nytimes.com/2018/08/23/us/randolph-county-georgia-voting.html.

FERNANDEZ, MANNY. "Texas' Voter ID Law Does Not Discriminate and Can

Stand, Appeals Panel Rules." *The New York Times*, 28 Apr. 2018, https://
www.nytimes.com/2018/04/27/us/texas-voter-id.html.

HABERMAN, CLYDE. "16 Years After Bush v. Gore, Still Wrestling With
Ballot-Box Rules." *The New York Times*, 22 Feb. 2016, https://www
.nytimes.com/2016/02/22/us/politics/16-years-after-bush-v-gore-still
-wrestling-with-ballot-box-rules.html.

HABERMAN, MAGGIE, AND JEREMY W. PETERS. "Donald Trump Campaign Seeks
'Voter Suppression,' Report Says, but It's Legal." *The New York Times*,
27 Oct. 2016, https://www.nytimes.com/2016/10/28/us/politics/donald
-trump-campaign-voter-suppression.html.

HAKIM, DANNY. "Before the Fights Over Recounts: An Election Day Vote
on Voting." *The New York Times*, 12 Nov. 2018, https://www.nytimes
.com/2018/11/12/us/politics/voting-rights-turnout-gerrymandering.html.

HAKIM, DANNY, AND MICHAEL WINES. " 'They Don't Really Want Us to Vote':
How Republicans Made It Harder." *The New York Times*, 3 Nov. 2018, https://
www.nytimes.com/2018/11/03/us/politics/voting-suppression-elections.html.

HERNDON, ASTEAD W. "Georgia Voting Begins Amid Accusations of Voter
Suppression." *The New York Times*, 19 Oct. 2018, https://www.nytimes
.com/2018/10/19/us/politics/georgia-voter-suppression.html.

HERNDON, ASTEAD W. "Stacey Abrams Will Not Run for President in 2020,
Focusing Instead on Fighting Voter Suppression." *The New York Times*,
13 Aug. 2019, https://www.nytimes.com/2019/08/13/us/politics/stacey
-abrams-fair-fight-2020.html.

HERNDON, ASTEAD W., AND TRIP GABRIEL. "Showdown in Georgia Governor's
Race Reflects a Larger Fight Over Voting Rights." *The New York Times*,
15 Oct. 2018, https://www.nytimes.com/2018/10/15/us/politics/georgia
-abrams-kemp-voting.html.

KROTOSZYNSKI, RONALD J., JR. "A Poll Tax by Another Name." *The New York
Times*, 14 Nov. 2016, https://www.nytimes.com/2016/11/14/opinion/a-poll
-tax-by-another-name.html.

LIPTAK, ADAM. "Justices Won't Revive Order Barring Voter Intimidation in
Ohio." *The New York Times*, 7 Nov. 2016, https://www.nytimes.com/2016
/11/08/us/politics/supreme-court-donald-trump-ohio.html.

LIPTAK, ADAM, AND MICHAEL WINES. "Strict North Carolina Voter ID Law
Thwarted After Supreme Court Rejects Case." *The New York Times*,
15 May 2017, https://www.nytimes.com/2017/05/15/us/politics/voter
-id-laws-supreme-court-north-carolina.html.

MAZZEI, PATRICIA. "Florida Limits Ex-Felon Voting, Prompting a Lawsuit and Cries of 'Poll Tax.'" *The New York Times*, 28 June 2019, https://www .nytimes.com/2019/06/28/us/florida-felons-voting-rights.html.

NEUMAN, WILLIAM. "400,000 New Yorkers Were Told Their Voter Registrations Were Inactive. Oops." *The New York Times*, 16 Oct. 2018, https://www .nytimes.com/2018/10/16/nyregion/inactive-voter-letter-nyc.html.

THE NEW YORK TIMES. "Vote. That's Just What They Don't Want You to Do." *The New York Times*, 14 Mar. 2018, https://www.nytimes.com/2018/03/10 /opinion/sunday/go-vote.html.

THE NEW YORK TIMES. "What the Supreme Court Doesn't Get About Racism." *The New York Times*, 2 Apr. 2018, https://www.nytimes.com/2018/04/02 /opinion/supreme-court-racism-suppression.html.

NORTH, ANNA. "Five Ways Republicans Are Threatening Voting Rights." *The New York Times*, 11 Nov. 2016, https://www.nytimes.com/2016 /11/07/opinion/five-ways-republicans-are-threatening-voting-rights .html.

PETERS, JEREMY W. "Spread of Early Voting Is Forging New Habits and Campaign Tactics." *The New York Times*, 11 Nov. 2016, https://www .nytimes.com/2016/11/08/us/early-voting-campaign-tactics.html.

PRICE, MELANYE. "Stacey Abrams Is Playing the Long Game for Our Democracy." *The New York Times*, 15 Aug. 2019, https://www.nytimes .com/2019/08/15/opinion/stacey-abrams-elections.html.

ROSENTHAL, ANDREW. "Maine Republicans Want to Get There (Vote Suppression) From Here (Vote Turnout)." *The New York Times*, 11 Nov. 2015, https://takingnote.blogs.nytimes.com/2011/11/15/maine-republicans -want-to-get-there-vote-suppression-from-here-vote-turnout/.

RUSSONELLO, GIOVANNI. "Voters Fear Their Ballot Won't Count, Poll Shows." *The New York Times*, 25 Oct. 2016, https://www.nytimes.com/2016/10/26 /us/politics/voter-fraud-poll.html.

STACK, LIAM. "Many Texas Voters Whose Citizenship Was Questioned Are in Fact Citizens." *The New York Times*, 29 Jan. 2019, https://www.nytimes .com/2019/01/29/us/texas-voter-citizenship-list.html.

STEVENS, MATT. "Tennessee Advances Bill That Could Make It Harder to Register New Voters." *The New York Times*, 16 Apr. 2019, https://www .nytimes.com/2019/04/16/us/politics/tennessee-voter-registration.html.

STOLBERG, SHERYL GAY, AND EMILY COCHRANE. "House Passes Voting Rights Bill Despite Near Unanimous Republican Opposition." *The New York*

Times, 6 Dec. 2019, https://www.nytimes.com/2019/12/06/us/politics
/house-voting-rights.html.

SZALAI, JENNIFER. "Whose Votes Really Count?" *The New York Times*,
12 Sept. 2018, https://www.nytimes.com/2018/09/12/books/review-one
-person-no-vote-carol-anderson.html.

TACKETT, MICHAEL, AND MICHAEL WINES. "Trump Disbands Commission on
Voter Fraud." *The New York Times*, 3 Jan. 2018, https://www.nytimes
.com/2018/01/03/us/politics/trump-voter-fraud-commission.html.

TURKEWITZ, JULIE. "For Native Americans, a 'Historic Moment' on the Path
to Power at the Ballot Box." *The New York Times*, 4 Jan. 2018, https://www
.nytimes.com/2018/01/04/us/native-american-voting-rights.html.

WANG, VIVIAN. "Why Deep Blue New York Is 'Voter Suppression Land.' "
The New York Times, 19 Dec. 2018, https://www.nytimes.com/2018/12/19
/nyregion/early-voting-reform-laws-ny.html.

WINES, MICHAEL. "Asked for Voters' Data, States Give Trump Panel a
Bipartisan 'No.' " *The New York Times*, 30 June 2017, https://www.nytimes
.com/2017/06/30/us/politics/kris-kobach-states-voter-fraud-data.html.

WINES, MICHAEL. "Kentucky Gives Voting Rights to Some 140,000 Former
Felons." *The New York Times*, 12 Dec. 2019, https://www.nytimes.com
/2019/12/12/us/kentucky-felons-voting-rights.html.

WINES, MICHAEL. "Some Republicans Acknowledge Leveraging Voter ID Laws
for Political Gain." *The New York Times*, 17 Sept. 2016, https://www.nytimes
.com/2016/09/17/us/some-republicans-acknowledge-leveraging-voter-id
-laws-for-political-gain.html.

WINES, MICHAEL. "The Student Vote Is Surging. So Are Efforts to Suppress
It." *The New York Times*, 24 Oct. 2019, https://www.nytimes.com/2019/10
/24/us/voting-college-suppression.html.

ZAVERI, MIHIR, AND JACEY FORTIN. "Russian Efforts Exploited Racial Divisions,
State of Black America Report Says." *The New York Times*, 6 May 2019,
https://www.nytimes.com/2019/05/06/us/russia-disinformation-black
-activists.html.

Index

This book is current up until the time of printing. For the most up-to-date reporting, visit www.nytimes.com.